Annotated Legal Documents on Islam in Europe: Italy

Annotated Legal Documents on Islam in Europe

VOLUME 9

The titles published in this series are listed at *brill.com/ldie*

Annotated Legal Documents on Islam in Europe:

Italy

Compiled and Annotated by

Stella Coglievina

BRILL

LEIDEN | BOSTON

Library of Congress Cataloging-in-Publication Data

Names: Coglievina, Stella, compiler.
Title: Annotated legal documents on Islam in Europe. Italy / compiled and annotated by Stella Coglievina.
Description: Leiden ; Boston : Brill, 2016. | Series: Annotated legal documents on Islam in Europe, ISSN 2214-1340 ; volume 9 | Includes bibliographical references and index.
Identifiers: LCCN 2015048067 | ISBN 9789004312357 (pbk. : alk. paper)
Subjects: LCSH: Muslims–Legal status, laws, etc.–Italy.
Classification: LCC KKH2467.M56 C64 2016 | DDC 342.4508/5297–dc23
LC record available at http://lccn.loc.gov/2015048067

Typeface for the Latin, Greek, and Cyrillic scripts: "Brill". See and download: brill.com/brill-typeface.

ISSN 2214-1340
ISBN 978-90-04-31235-7 (paperback)

This book is printed on acid-free paper and produced in a sustainable manner.

Printed by Printforce, the Netherlands

Contents

Foreword by the Editors

This is the ninth volume in the series *Annotated Legal Documents on Islam in Europe*. The publication of this series responds to the widespread lack of sound information about the legal status of Islam in Europe. In principle, this information is easily available to those who are willing to make the effort and know enough about the subject to ask the right questions of the digital search engines. But that requires both expertise and effort, and it takes place in an environment where the public political debate on Islam in many European countries is characterised by increasing concern and fear. Islam has come to be broadly perceived as a security issue rather than a religion like others in Europe. But the concern has also moved into the legal field, most markedly, of course, with discussions about limitations on Muslim female dress enacted in France, Belgium, Italy and Spain, or the ban on building minarets on mosques in Switzerland, or restrictions on building mosques in Austria. At the same time, in a number of European states like Austria and Germany, legislation is enacted and state treaties are negotiated which aim to establish a stable and reliable basis for Muslim life and organisation. Even so, such measures are under scrutiny by an increasingly sceptical European public, sometimes ignoring the legal principles of secularity, not least the demands of state neutrality towards and equal treatment of all religions and beliefs regardless of numbers of adherents or public reputation.

In addition, the religious status and rights of Muslims in the various European countries differ significantly, due to different historical developments regarding the organisation of the relations between the state and religions. Furthermore, while in some states laws regulating such matters introduced decades ago are still in force and have to be re-interpreted in the face of a 'newcomer' religion, others have introduced new laws which consider the increasing religious plurality within Europe. Despite the common legal and political foundations constructed since 1945 in instruments such as the European Convention on Human Rights and the more recently accumulated legislation of the European Union, this closer look reveals remarkable differences due to the extent of separating state and religion or establishing co-operative structures. In some countries Islam has an officially recognised status which in several cases originated in the first half of the 20th century. In other countries no such recognition of any religion is available even if informal ways of favouring one religion over another may exist. Since 1990 especially, European courts have moved to equalise the status of Islam with that of other religions in the practical exercise of religious freedom in various countries. Particular practices regarded as core religious obligations—in the case of Muslims dress codes and practices such as male circumcision, access to correctly slaughtered meat and otherwise *halal* food, free time for the main periods of worship and religious festivals, and the right to build mosques—can be controversial in some countries while less so in others. In the course of the ongoing process of self-organisation and the participation of Muslims in civil societies and their cooperation with the state, children's access to Islamic religious instruction or the education of Muslim theologians can be achieved in cooperation with the state education systems in some countries, while in others the community must rely on its own arrangements. The practically pressing issue of financing the religious infrastructure is still far from being settled in many countries.

The aim of this series is to make this legislation available to both the interested researcher and the practising lawyer. Altogether the series is expected to comprise 32 volumes, one for each of the 28 countries of the European Union plus Norway and Switzerland, and a volume each dealing with the European Union (treaties, directives and decisions of the Court of Justice of the European Communities) and the European Court of Human Rights. Excerpts of relevant legislation will be introduced and summarised by the volume compiler, and where court cases have provided significant interpretation of the law they will also be referred to. The legislation itself is reproduced in the original language, as the editors and the publisher agreed early on in the preparation of the series that any attempt to translate legislation into English would be unsatisfactory and could be misleading. The annotation by the compiler should give sufficient guidance to users to allow a decision as to whether to arrange a translation for their specific purposes.

While there is in many countries legislation explicitly referring to aspects of Islam, most often regarding official recognition or to do with education, in other countries there is none. Italy is one of those countries where a form of official recognition does exist, although until the present it has only once been applied to an Islamic organisation.

An attempt has been made to ensure that the volumes are structured in as similar a manner as possible. The starting point for this has been the thematic organisation of the first six volumes of the *Yearbook of Muslims in Europe* which Brill has published annually since 2009 (the *Yearbook* is being restructured from vol. 7 published in 2015). But it has only been a starting point, and in each volume the compiler and the editors have agreed on the structure which makes most sense for the legislation of the country concerned. Normally one member of the editorial group takes responsibility for discussing the structure and compilation of each volume with the compiler: in this instance we are grateful to Prof. Silvio Ferrari, University of Milan. We are also grateful to Kate

Elliott for the care shown in copy editing the volume. The idea for this project came from the publisher, where Nicolette van der Hoek and Nienke Brienen-Moolenaar have played an invaluable role in ensuring that the project has maintained its momentum. As editors, we appreciate how much their expertise contributes to ensuring that a project like this can run smoothly.

It is in the nature of such a project that each volume, if left as it stands, will gradually become out of date as new legislation and cases appear. It is the intention of the editors and publishers in due course to make the contents available on-line in a form which will permit regular updating.

The Editors
November 2015

General Introduction

Italy is a predominantly Catholic country: there are clear historical ties to the Holy See and the great majority of Italians consider themselves as belonging to the Catholic Church, even if a small percentage actually habitually practises religion.[1] Christian roots are evident in Italian traditions and in cultural and artistic heritage; Christianity has also shaped many legal instruments and customs. Catholicism has enjoyed special legal treatment for many centuries, and some pieces of the legislation in force still recognise the role of Christian traditions and assure privileges to the (nominally) Catholic majority.[2]

The presence of Islam is quite recent and mainly due to the immigration flows that have taken place in Europe, especially since the late 1970s.[3] Immigrants of Islamic origin have for a long while been considered to be temporary workers; moreover, they have often been identified through their national rather than religious affiliation.[4] Thus Islam was almost absent in the public sphere until recently and no significant changes have been introduced into Italian legislation in order to take into account the religious needs of the Muslim community. The legal framework regarding fundamental rights and state–religion relations in Italy includes different tools for the protection of religious freedom and the legal treatment of religious minorities. Many articles of the Italian Constitution take religious freedom into account, both from an individual and from a collective point of view. The attitude of Italian public authorities

1 Ferrari, Alessandro and Ferrari, Silvio, "Religion and the Secular State, The Italian Case" (Italian National Reports to Washington 2010), in *The Cardozo Electronic Law Bulletin*, vol. 16 (1), Special Issue, available at http://cardozolawbulletin.blogspot.it/search/label/16 (last accessed 19 May 2015).

2 For an overview in English see Ventura, Marco, *Religion and Law in Italy*, Alphen aan den Rijn: Wolters Kluwer International, 2013.

3 Norman Doe, *Law and Religion in Europe: A Comparative Introduction*, Oxford: Oxford University Press, 2011, pp. 10 ff.

4 See the analysis of the situation of Muslims in Italy in the early 2000s by Allievi, Stefano, *Islam italiano. Viaggio nella seconda religione del paese*, Torino: Einaudi, 2003; Pacini, Andrea, *I musulmani in Italia*, Cestim 2001 at http://www.cestim.it/argomenti/02islam/02islam-relazione-pacini.pdf (last accessed 19 May 2015). See also Ferrari, Alessandro, "Islam in Italy: The 'Ghost' Religion (A 'non-religion' in a 'religious country')", *Annuaire Droit et Religions*, vol. 8, 2015–2016, pp. 365–382; Conti, Bartolomeo, *Towards a pluralistic society: Good practices in the integration and social inclusion of Muslims in Italian cities*, Florence: EUI-Open Society Institute, 2013, available at http://www.eui.eu/Projects/ReligioWest/Documents/Publications/REPORT2013CONTI.pdf (last accessed 19 May 2015).

and of civic society towards religions has usually been favourable and tolerant; therefore, the religious needs of Muslims have often been accommodated through informal agreements, especially in employment or with regard to students' religious practices in schools (dietary rules, religious attires such as the hijab, etc.).

After the more recent immigration flows in the 1990s and family reunifications, Islamic communities have started to settle in Italy and to create organisations and associations to satisfy religious needs.[5] Today, Islam is the second largest religious group in Italy: according to the latest estimates, there are between 1.5 and 2.2 million Muslims in the country.[6] Due to the citizenship rules, many Muslims in Italy are still registered as residents without Italian citizenship, but there is a growing number of children of immigrants born in Italy and young Muslims with weak ties to their countries of origin.[7] Therefore, the representation of Islamic needs is stronger than in the past, as different organisations are more structured and Muslims are more practised in the use of mass media and more active in the social life, in universities, political organisations, etc. The public presence of Islam is more visible, also due to many different places of worship and associations, often with open relations with the civic community and with public authorities.[8]

---

5 Among the numerous analyses of immigration and Islam in Italy see Open Society Institute (OSI), *The Situation of Muslims in Italy*, Open Society, 2002 (available at http://www.cestim.it/argomenti/02islam/osi%20-%20muslims%20in%20italy.pdf, last accessed 19 May 2015); Allievi, Stefano, "Sociology of a Newcomer: Muslim Migration to Italy—Religious Visibility, Cultural and Political Reactions", *Immigrants & Minorities: Historical Studies in Ethnicity, Migration and Diaspora*, vol. 22, 2–3, 2003, 141–154; Guolo, Renzo, "Attori sociali e processi di rappresentanza nell'islam italiano", in Saint-Blancat, Chantal (ed.), *L'islam in Italia. Una presenza plurale*, Rome: Edizioni Lavoro, 1999, pp. 67ff.

6 There is no official census of religious communities in Italy; according to the statistics, the number of Muslims, who are mostly Sunnis, is between 1.5 and 2.2 million (2.5% to 3.5% of the total population of about 60 million). For estimates of the Muslim population in Italy see *Le religioni in Italia*, directed by Massimo Introvigne and Pierluigi Zoccatelli, available at http://www.cesnur.com/lislam-e-i-movimenti-di-matrice-islamica-in-italia/lislam-sunnita-unintroduzione/. See also Coglievina, Stella, "Italy", in *Yearbook of Muslims in Europe*, in Nielsen, Jorgen et al. (eds.), Leiden: Brill, 2014, vol. 6, pp. 334ff. (general overview on data and bibliography).

7 About the presence of young Muslims see Frisina, Annalisa, *Giovani Musulmani d'Italia*, Rome: Carocci, 2007.

8 Recent data about mosques and Islamic associations in Italy are published in *Islam e integrazione in Italia*, edited by Angelucci, Antonio, Bombardieri, Maria, and Tacchini, Davide, Venice: Marsilio, 2014.

However, Islam is still perceived as a foreign reality in Italy and often connected to immigration, with related social problems.[9] From a legal point of view, some rights of the Muslim community—particularly from a collective point of view—are still difficult to accommodate.[10] The Islamic community in Italy is significantly diverse, both from the ethnic/national point of view and from a cultural/religious one. Therefore, many different organisations and associations exist, with different representation and different visibility in the public sphere.[11] The absence of a unitary organisation is one of the factors that have hitherto blocked the opportunity to reach an agreement with the state, which is one of the main instruments establishing the legal treatment of a religious community.[12] Indeed, a system of agreements between state and religious

9 Ferrari, Alessandro, "Islam in Italy: The 'Ghost' Religion (A 'non-religion' in a 'religious country')".

10 The results of recent research about the different aspects of religious rights and Islam in Italy are presented in the recent volume *Comunità islamiche in Italia. Identità e forme giuridiche*, edited by Cardia, Carlo and Dalla Torre, Giuseppe, Turin: Giappichelli Editore, 2015. About the difficulties of managing the legal treatment of Islam in Italy see also Aluffi Beck-Peccoz, Roberta, "The legal treatment of the Muslim minority in Italy", in Aluffi Beck-Peccoz, Roberta and Zincone, Giovanna (eds), *The Legal Treatment of Islamic Minorities in Europe*, Leuven: Peeters, 2004; Ferrari, Silvio and Bradney, Anthony (eds.), *Islam and European Legal Systems*, Farnham: Ashgate, 2000.

11 Bibliography on the characteristics of Islam in Italy (which is significantly diverse, both from an ethnic and from a religious point of view) and about the different Muslim associations is very abundant. See, among the most recent publications, Toronto, James A., "Islam Italiano: Prospects for Integration of Muslims in Italy's Religious Landscape", *Journal of Muslim Minority Affairs*, vol. 28, no. 1, 2008, pp. 61–82; Allievi, Stefano, *I musulmani e la società italiana. Percezioni reciproche, conflitti culturali, trasformazioni sociali*, Milan: Franco Angeli, 2009; Bombardieri, Maria, *Moschee d'Italia*, Bologna: EMI, 2011; Conti, Bartolomeo, "Les musulmans en Italie entre crise identitaire et réponses islamistes", *Revue Européenne des Migrations Internationales*, vol. 27, no. 2, 2011, pp. 183–201; Saint-Blancat, Chantal, "Italy", in Cesari, Jocelyne (ed.), *The Oxford Handbook of European Islam*, Oxford: Oxford University Press 2014, pp. 288 ff.

12 Casuscelli, Giuseppe, "La rappresentanza e l'intesa", in Ferrari, Alessandro (ed.), *Islam in Europa/Islam in Italia tra diritto e società*, Bologna: Il Mulino, 2008, pp. 285–322; Alicino, Francesco, *La legislazione sulla base di intesa. I test delle religioni "altre" e degli ateismi*, Bari: Cacucci, 2013, pp. 112 ff.; Cardia, Carlo, "Le ragioni di una ricerca. Le originalità dell'islam, le difficoltà dell'integrazione", in *Comunità islamiche in Italia. Identità e forme giuridiche*, pp. 3–27 (available at http://www.olir.it/areetematiche/libri/documents/01-cardia.pdf); Cavana, Paolo, "Islam e sistema delle fonti in Italia", *ivi*, pp. 45–74. About the attempts to reach an agreement (*intesa*) and related legal problems see also Ferrari, Silvio (ed.), *Musulmani in Italia: la condizione giuridica delle comunità islamiche*, Bologna: Il Mulino, 2000.

denominations characterises Italy: in the past, only the Concordat between the Catholic Church and the Italian State was in force; with the Republican Constitution of 1948 the "concordat" system was extended to other religions.[13] Article 8.3 of the Constitution allows religious denominations to conclude bilateral agreements (*intese*) with the Government with the aim of regulating their relations with the state. The agreements concluded hitherto have defined the specific conditions for the exercise of religious freedom in some areas, giving religious denominations the ability—among other rights—to receive public funds, to see religious marriages recognised, and to enjoy the accommodation of different religious needs.

Even if the *intesa* is not the only legal tool for the protection of religious freedom, groups without agreements—including Islam—are subject to the 1929 legislation on religious freedom and cannot enjoy some specific privileges and legal treatment.[14] Other pieces of state legislation can also grant rights to religious communities (for example legislation on religious rights in some public places, including the ability to organise chaplaincy; legislation on associations and the right to assemble and freedom of expression, etc.). However, with regard to Islam some problems emerge. On the one hand, the legal treatment of religious groups is often shaped on the Christian model and it is difficult to apply to Muslim communities.[15] On the other hand, especially in recent years, dealing with Islam is often seen as a question of immigration and security, as many immigrants and refugees, landing in Italy through the Mediterranean, are Muslims. The confusion between immigration issues and religious diversity issues is frequent, both in the public discourse and among the policy makers. Thus, the legal treatment of Islam sometimes overlaps with the problems linked to immigration, social cohesion, welfare, and security.[16] This situation, together with the economic crisis and the hostility to immigration in some parts of the population, makes the management of different Islamic needs more con-

---

13 See chapter 1. For an overview in English see Ventura, Marco, "Religion and law in dialogue: Covenantal and non-covenantal cooperation of State and religions in Italy", in Puza, Richard and Doe, Norman (eds.), *Religion and law in dialogue: Covenantal and non-covenantal cooperation between State and Religion in Europe*, European Consortium for Church-State Research Conference, Leuven: Peeters, 2006, pp. 115–129.

14 Ferrari, Alessandro, *La libertà religiosa in Italia. Un percorso incompiuto*, Rome: Carocci, 2012, pp. 95ff.; Alicino, Francesco, *La legislazione sulla base di intesa*, pp. 109ff.

15 Ferrari, Alessandro, "Islam in Italy: The 'Ghost' Religion (A 'non-religion' in a 'religious country')".

16 For a general overview of the public perceptions and political discourse on Islam and immigration in Italy see Saint-Blancat, Chantal, "Italy".

troversial and debated.[17] The security argument is also used as international fundamentalism is rising.[18]

As a consequence of these factors, Italian government and public authorities are not taking sufficiently into account the need to provide clear legal treatment for Muslim groups and for their religious rights. Often, Muslims' requests are accommodated with a day-to-day approach, without an overall perspective, simply looking at the compelling and urgent necessities.[19]

An analysis of the legal framework of the status of Islam in Italy reflects this situation. First of all, specific legislation about the legal situation of Islam in Italy is very scarce, if not entirely lacking. As already said, no Islamic organisation has signed an agreement with the state in accordance with Article 8.3 of the Constitution. Therefore, there is no specific legislation concerning the status of the Muslim community and its relations with the state; a few provisions deal with the legal personality of one of the Italian Muslim organisations and the institution of consultative bodies, created with the aim of developing state–Islam relations.[20]

Secondly, the provisions on religious freedom only rarely explicitly consider Islamic needs (one of the few examples is the legislation on ritual slaughter). Moreover, the only general Act on religious freedom in force is an old piece of legislation (Act n. 1159 of 1929), which applies to religious denominations not having an agreement with the state. The Islamic community can refer to the 1929 Act in order to enjoy some special rights granted to religious groups. However, problems emerge in this regard. The Act of 1929 often refers to religious

17 This is evident, for example, in the case of building mosques. See Ferrari, Silvio, "Le moschee in Italia tra ordine pubblico e libertà religiosa", in *Quattordicesimo rapporto sulle migrazioni 2008*, Milano: Franco Angeli, 2009, pp. 219–236; Allievi, Stefano, *Conflicts over Mosques in Europe. Policy issues and trends*, London: Alliance Publishing Trust, 2009 (at http://www.nef-europe.org/wp-content/uploads/2013/03/Conflicts-over-mosques_NEF-RelDem-RELIGION-MOSQUES-Final-1.pdf, last accessed on 26 January 2015). The aim of security protection emerges also in the proposals for regulating burqa issues: see Ferrari, Alessandro, "A Besieged Right: Religious Freedom and the Italian War on the Burqa and the Niqab", in Ferrari, Alessandro and Pastorelli, Sabrina [you have used full first names after the patronymic before. Please do so here] (eds.), *The Burqa Affair Across Europe*, Farnham: Ashgate, 2013, pp. 37–58.

18 Coglievina, Stella, "Italy", in Scharbrodt Oliver et al. (eds.), *Yearbook of Muslims in Europe*, vol. 7, Leiden: Brill, Leiden 2015.

19 Ferrari, Alessandro, "Islam in Italy: The 'Ghost' Religion (A 'non-religion' in a 'religious country')"; Naso, Paolo and Salvarani, Brunetto (eds), *Un cantiere senza progetto. L'Italia delle Religioni. Rapporto 2012*, Bologna: EMI, 2012.

20 See chapters 1 and 2.

entities with legal personality, but among the many different Muslim organisations in Italy only one has it. For this reason, and due to the obsolescence of many of the 1929 provisions, this legislation does not respond to a number of specific requests of the Islamic community.[21]

Thirdly, various provisions are applied to Islamic practices and activities, but they refer to religion only indirectly. For example, many Muslim organisations are created and regulated according to the common legislation on associations.[22] The application of legislation on other rights (freedom of association, provisions on cultural diversity, etc.) to religious communities poses problems with regard to the specific characteristics and needs of the right of religious freedom.[23]

Therefore, the legal documents on Islam presented in this volume are mainly general documents about religious freedom or, more broadly, about freedom of association or expression which apply to Islam. In addition, we have considered some provisions about relations with foreign Muslim countries (for example for the recognition of marriages concluded abroad[24]), as often Muslims are foreigners without Italian citizenship, and about racial discrimination,[25] often linked to the national and ethnic origin of Muslims residents. The documents published here are not numerous, as no specific legislation on Islam exists. Moreover, the accommodation of Muslims' religious needs is often made through informal agreements, without any specific legal provision.

In the arrangements about religious needs, local and regional authorities can have a role too. The Italian Constitution gives some competences to Regions (Art. 117) and administrative competence to the municipalities; mayors can also pass secondary legislation on some specific matters. Among the matters reserved to local entities, some also concern religious freedom or other related issues.[26] Thus, some regional Acts or municipalities' decisions can be relevant

---

21 See Ferrari, Alessandro, "Islam in Italy: The 'Ghost' Religion (A 'non-religion' in a 'religious country')".

22 See chapter 1.4.

23 Ferrari, Alessandro, "Islam in Italy: The 'Ghost' Religion (A 'non-religion' in a 'religious country')".

24 See chapter 15.

25 See for example chapter 4.

26 About the legislation on religious freedom at the local level see Chizzoniti, Antonio G. (ed.), *Religione e autonomie locali. La tutela della libertà religiosa nei territori di Cremona, Lodi e Piacenza*, Tricase: Libellula Edizioni, 2014; Angeletti, Silvia, "Le attività delle comunità islamiche a livello locale. Alcune considerazioni alla luce dei risultati della ricerca", in Cardia, Carlo and Dalla Torre, Giuseppe (eds), *Comunità islamiche in Italia*, pp. 149–174.

for understanding the legal treatment of Islam (though not explicitly referring to it). It would be impossible to publish every legal document approved at the local level and concerning (directly or indirectly) religious matters: this volume presents only some examples.

Wherever it was possible, we have referred also to relevant Italian case law in order to illustrate the interpretation of particular legal issues.

The main electronic sources used in this volume are www.normattiva.it (an updated database of Italian primary and secondary legislation, which includes amendments to each document) and www.olir.it (a database of legislation and case law on religious freedom issues). The information included in this volume was last updated in May 2015.

CHAPTER 1

Status of Religious Communities

1.1 Constitutional Guarantees

The Italian Constitution was approved in 1947 and came into force in 1948. It introduced a Republican legal order and it is based on the principles of democracy, equality and freedom. Several Articles mention freedom of religion and relationships between the state and religious denominations.

Freedom of religion is proclaimed by Article 19, which guarantees both individual and collective freedom, the right to profess a religion and to perform rites, both in public and in private.

Together with the right to freedom of religion, Article 3 prescribes the equality of all citizens before the law, irrespective of religious convictions, and the duty of the state to provide for effective equality. Therefore, every person is free to have and profess a belief on equal conditions.

According to Article 19, religious freedom can be limited only when it interferes with public morality (*buon costume*); moreover, restrictions can only be imposed on rites once performed. Case law has underlined that the constitutional principles prevent an *a priori* control on the practices or characteristics of a religion.[1]

This type of control is clearly prohibited also if one considers the principle of independence and autonomy of religious denominations before the state. This principle can be read in Articles 7.1 and 8.2 of the Constitution, regarding respectively the sovereignty of the Catholic Church and the autonomy of other religious denominations. Every religion is free to act in Italy, and the state shall not interfere with their organisation or dogmas. Beyond this principle, Articles 7 and 8 proclaim the freedom of all religious denominations (they are "equally free before the law", according to Art. 8.1) and establish a system of agreements regulating the relationships between the Catholic Church and

1 See Constitutional Court, judgment n. 45 of 18 March 1957 (available at http://www.giurcost.org/decisioni/1957/0045s-57.html, last accessed 1 February 2015). This has been important for the debate about Islam, where many have hoped for control over its religious principles that can sometimes be seen as contrary to the Italian legal order. On freedom of religion and its limits see Casuscelli, Giuseppe (ed.), *Nozioni di Diritto ecclesiastico*, Torino: Giappichelli, 2015, pp. 113 ff. With regard to Islam see Ferrari, Silvio, "Le questioni normative", in Ferrari, Alessandro (ed.), *Islam in Europa/Islam in Italia tra diritto e società*, Bologna: Il Mulino, 2008, pp. 84 ff.

the state (Art. 7.2) and between the state and other religions (Art. 8.3). This is one of the main characteristics of the Italian model of relationships between the state and religions: looking at the Constitution, the instrument of bilateral agreements is the ideal tool to guarantee religious freedom, especially at the collective level.[2] The Constitution does not mention the principle of secularism (*laicità*) or neutrality, that has been proclaimed by the Constitutional Court in 1989 as a supreme principle of the Italian legal order.[3]

Article 117 of the Italian Constitution, distributing the legislative competence between the state and the Regions, distinguishes between exclusive competences of the state, concurrent competences, and exclusive competences of the Regions. Relationships between state and religious denominations are attributed to the exclusive competence of the state (Art. 117.2, letter c); according to scholars, this refers only to the state–religions relationships at the level of agreements with the state and other issues at the central level, while Regions are not prevented from dialogue or concluding other agreements with religious groups at the local level.[4] Moreover, Regions have concurrent legislative competence in several areas related to religious issues (Art. 117.3 refers, for example, to education, cultural heritage, urban management).

Costituzione della Repubblica Italiana (Constitution) 22 dicembre 1947[5]

Art. 3

1. Tutti i cittadini hanno pari dignità sociale e sono eguali davanti alla legge, senza distinzione di sesso, di razza, di lingua, di religione, di opinioni politiche, di condizioni personali e sociali.

2 As a matter of fact, this instrument has posed some problems, especially with "new" religious communities recently settled in Italy. Islam has not reached the conclusion of an agreement with the state, as we will see in the following paragraphs.

3 Constitutional Court, judgment n. 203/1989 (at http://www.olir.it/documenti/?documento=370). The principle of *laicità* does not mean indifference of the State towards religions, but neutrality; it requires an equal promotion of all religions, without interference of the State in their activities. The Court inferred this principle from the other abovementioned articles of the Constitution.

4 See Pastori, Giorgio, "Regioni e confessioni religiose nel nuovo ordinamento costituzionale", in *Quaderni di diritto e politica ecclesiastica*, 2003, n. 1, 3–12; Cavana, Paolo, "Islam e sistema delle fonti in Italia", in Cardia, Carlo and Dalla Torre, Giuseppe, *Comunità islamiche in Italia*, pp. 50ff.

5 The Constitution has been in force since 1 January 1948. Text available at http://www.quirinale.it/qrnw/statico/costituzione/pdf/Costituzione.pdf, and translation in English at http://en.camera.it/application/xmanager/projects/camera_eng/file/costituzione_EN_dicembre2014.pdf (last accessed 26 January 2015).

2. È compito della Repubblica rimuovere gli ostacoli di ordine economico e sociale, che, limitando di fatto la libertà e l'eguaglianza dei cittadini, impediscono il pieno sviluppo della persona umana e l'effettiva partecipazione di tutti i lavoratori all'organizzazione politica, economica e sociale del Paese.

Art. 7
1. Lo Stato e la Chiesa cattolica sono, ciascuno nel proprio ordine, indipendenti e sovrani.
2. I loro rapporti sono regolati dai Patti Lateranensi. Le modificazioni dei Patti, accettate dalle due parti, non richiedono procedimento di revisione costituzionale.

Art. 8
1. Tutte le confessioni religiose sono egualmente libere davanti alla legge.
2. Le confessioni religiose diverse dalla cattolica hanno diritto di organizzarsi secondo i propri statuti, in quanto non contrastino con l'ordinamento giuridico italiano.
3. I loro rapporti con lo Stato sono regolati per legge sulla base di intese con le relative rappresentanze.

Art. 19
Tutti hanno diritto di professare liberamente la propria fede religiosa in qualsiasi forma, individuale o associata, di farne propaganda e di esercitarne in privato o in pubblico il culto, purché non si tratti di riti contrari al buon costume.

Art. 117
1. La potestà legislativa è esercitata dallo Stato e dalle Regioni nel rispetto della Costituzione, nonché dei vincoli derivanti dall'ordinamento comunitario e dagli obblighi internazionali.
2. Lo Stato ha legislazione esclusiva nelle seguenti materie:
[...]
b) immigrazione;
c) rapporti tra la Repubblica e le confessioni religiose
[...]
3. Sono materie di legislazione concorrente quelle relative a:
[...]
tutela e sicurezza del lavoro; istruzione, salva l'autonomia delle istituzioni scolastiche e con esclusione della istruzione e della formazione professionale; professioni; ricerca scientifica e tecnologica e sostegno all'innovazione per i

> settori produttivi; tutela della salute; alimentazione; ordinamento sportivo; protezione civile; governo del territorio;
> […]
> valorizzazione dei beni culturali e ambientali e promozione e organizzazione di attività culturali;
> […]
> Nelle materie di legislazione concorrente spetta alle Regioni la potestà legislativa, salvo che per la determinazione dei principi fondamentali, riservata alla legislazione dello Stato.
> 4. Spetta alle Regioni la potestà legislativa in riferimento ad ogni materia non espressamente riservata alla legislazione dello Stato.

1.2 Legal Recognition of Churches and Religious Communities

As has already been said, religious denominations are free to act in the Italian legal order, in accordance with Articles 7 and 8 of the Constitution. In particular, Article 8.1 states that "all religious denominations are equally free before the law". It is worth noting that neither the Constitution nor Italian law defines what a "religious denomination" (*confessione religiosa*) is.[6] Moreover, there is no system of registration of religious groups, which are not obliged to have a particular legal status or recognition. Article 20 of the Italian Constitution states that religious communities shall not be subject to limitations in their legal capabilities or legal status.

Historically speaking, in Italy there has always been a great difference between the legal status of the Catholic Church and the situation of other denominations. The Catholic Church has an undisputed legal personality, connected to the international legal status of the Holy See and to its presence in Italy through the centuries. Thus its legal personality has never been formally recognised, but it was implicit in the provisions of the Lateran Pacts of 1929 and enshrined by Article 7 of the Constitution, which proclaims the sovereignty and independence of the Catholic Church.

Other religious denominations have the right (but they are not obliged) to have their own statute in accordance with Article 8.2 of the Constitution, and they can stipulate an agreement with the state, in accordance with Article 8.3 of the Constitution. Their legal status is not properly defined by Italian law,

6 Cf. Finocchiaro, Francesco, *Diritto ecclesiastico*, Bologna: Zanichelli, 2012, pp. 71ff.

but we can find relevant provisions in Act n. 1159 of 1929 (the so-called "Act on admitted cults"[7]) and in Royal Decree n. 289 of 1930, implementing the Act.

More specifically, the 1929 Act does not provide for a register of religious denominations, nor for the recognition of religious communities as such: its Article 2 provides for the recognition of the legal personality of the bodies (*enti*) of a religious denomination. According to Article 2 and to the provisions of Royal Decree n. 289 of 1930, religious entities shall be recognised if the state can acknowledge their religious character and purposes. After an evaluation of their statutes and the advice of the Council of State, their legal personality can be recognised through a decree of the President of the Republic.[8]

It is important to underline that this sort of registration is not compulsory, but it has been considered a necessary condition in order to establish an agreement (*intesa*) with the state.[9] The agreements are important tools for granting rights and privileges to religious communities in Italy (for example, for access to public funding), so this situation has given rise to different status for religions that have their bodies recognised, for religions with agreements, and for religions that have no agreement or any type of recognition. Moreover, legal personality is needed for the implementation of some rights (for example the ability of religious denominations to create private religious schools: see section 7.3 below), and it normally makes easier the recognition of privileges or facilitations that have been established for religious entities (fiscal and organisational special rules; the ability to establish relationships with public authorities, for example for building places of worship, etc.[10]).

Islam is among the denominations without agreement and without recognition under Article 2 of the 1929 Act, except for the Islamic Cultural Centre in Rome (see section 2.2.1). Indeed, the system of recognition and agreements has created some difficulties for Islam, because normally Muslim communities in Italy are not organised like other religious denominations (e.g. Christian churches), with a hierarchical structure, bodies, entities and ministers

7 The 1929 Act was passed at the same time as the Lateran Pacts, with the aim of regulating the status of non-Catholic religions. Since the passing of the Constitution, it has been amended by the Constitutional Court on several occasions in order to avoid conflicts with constitutional guarantees.

8 In the procedure of recognition, the government (i.e. the Council of Ministers) shall give its opinion, so it has a discretionary power in this procedure. In consequence, the recognition of religious communities under the 1929 legislation is not always easy.

9 Vitali, Enrico and Chizzoniti, Antonio G., *Diritto ecclesiastico. Manuale breve*, Milan: Giuffrè, 2015, pp. 52.

10 See further, chapters 2 and 5.

(persons in charge of worship and/or responsible for the organisation of the religious body).[11]

In any case, it is important to bear in mind that constitutional principles do not oblige religions to register, nor to have a statute, nor to enter into an agreement with the state: they are all free to act in Italy. Religious denominations can also be identified through case law, without the need for formal registration under the 1929 legislation.[12] This kind of "recognition" does not give them the privileges reserved for religious bodies with legal personality, but it is limited to acknowledging the presence and the freedom of an organised group with religious aims.

Costituzione della Repubblica Italiana

Art. 20
Il carattere ecclesiastico e il fine di religione o di culto d'una associazione od istituzione non possono essere causa di speciali limitazioni legislative, né di speciali gravami fiscali per la sua costituzione, capacità giuridica e ogni forma di attività.

Legge 24 giugno 1929, n. 1159, ***Disposizioni sull'esercizio dei culti ammessi nello Stato e sul matrimonio celebrato davanti ai ministri dei culti medesimi***[13]

Art. 1
Sono ammessi nello Stato culti diversi dalla religione cattolica apostolica e romana, purché non professino principi e non seguano riti contrari all'ordine pubblico o al buon costume. L'esercizio, anche pubblico di tali culti è libero.

11 On the difficulties of applying these categories to Islam see, among others, Cardia, Carlo, "Le ragioni di una ricerca. Le originalità dell'islam, le difficoltà dell'integrazione", in *Comunità islamiche in Italia. Identità e forme giuridiche*, pp. 22 ff. (available at http://www.olir.it/areetematiche/libri/documents/01-cardia.pdf); Floris, Pierangela, "Comunità islamiche e lacune normative. L'ente che non c'è: l'associazione con fine di religione e di culto", *ivi*, pp. 75–96; Ferrari, Alessandro, "Libertà religiosa e nuove presenze confessionali (ortodossi e islamici): tra cieca deregulation e super-specialità, ovvero del difficile spazio per la differenza religiosa", in *Stato, Chiese e pluralismo confessionale*, online journal (www.statoechiese.it), 4 July 2011, pp. 11 ff.

12 See, for example, judgment of the Constitutional Court, n. 195 of 27 April 1993; judgment of the Court of Cassation n. 1329 of 22 October 1997.

13 http://www.olir.it/documenti/?documento=199 (last accessed 26 January 2015).

Art. 2
Gli istituti di culti diversi dalla religione dello Stato possono essere eretti in ente morale, con decreto del Presidente della Repubblica su proposta del Ministro dell'Interno, uditi il Consiglio di Stato e il Consiglio dei ministri. Norme speciali per l'esercizio della vigilanza e del controllo da parte dello Stato possono inoltre essere stabilite nel decreto di erezione in ente morale.

Regio Decreto 28 febbraio 1930, n. 289—*Norme per l'attuazione della legge 24 giugno 1929, n. 1159/1929, sui culti ammessi nello Stato e per il coordinamento di essa con le altre leggi dello Stato*[14]
(*Gazzetta ufficiale della Repubblica Italiana* n. 87 del 12 aprile 1930)

Art. 10
L'erezione in ente morale degli istituti dei culti diversi dalla religione dello Stato può essere chiesta da qualsiasi interessato con domanda diretta al Ministro dell'Interno.
La domanda è presentata all'ufficio di culto presso la prefettura e deve essere corredata del testo dello statuto dell'ente da cui risultino lo scopo, gli organi dell'amministrazione, le norme di funzionamento di esso, i mezzi finanziari dei quali dispone per il raggiungimento dei propri fini.
Con il decreto di erezione può stabilirsi che il legittimo rappresentante dell'ente sia cittadino italiano.
In ogni caso, però, il legittimo rappresentante dell'ente deve avere il domicilio nel regno.

Art. 11
Ove lo statuto di un istituto dei culti diversi dalla religione dello Stato non vi provveda, si deve nel decreto di erezione dell'istituto stesso in ente morale disporre circa le finalità alle quali saranno devoluti i beni dell'ente, in caso di estinzione del medesimo per qualsiasi causa.
Di regola devono essere preferite le finalità di istruzione, di educazione o di beneficenza a favore dei naturali del luogo in cui l'ente svolge la propria azione.

Art. 12
Relativamente agli atti compiuti nell'interesse di istituti, eretti in ente morale, dai culti ammessi nello Stato, il fine di culto è, a tutti gli effetti tributari, equiparato a quello di beneficenza e di istruzione.

---

14 Text with amendments is available at http://www.olir.it/documenti/?documento=234 (last accessed 26 January 2015).

> Art. 13
> Oltre alle norme speciali stabilite nel decreto di erezione in ente morale, gli istituti dei culti diversi dalla religione dello Stato sono soggetti alla vigilanza ed alla tutela governativa.
> Tutte le attribuzioni spettanti allo Stato sugli istituti sopra menzionati sono esercitate dal Ministro dell'Interno e dagli organi dal medesimo dipendenti.

1.3 Registered Religious Communities

Having said that there is no official register of churches and religious communities in Italy, and that recognition under Act n. 1159/1929 is not compulsory, it is worth noting that the legislation of 1929–1930 gives some particular rights to the religious bodies that have been recognised. For example, they may benefit from special protection of their autonomy and internal organisation, their ministers can access public structures for chaplaincy services in an easier way, etc.

In any case, religious communities can act in the Italian State as associations (under public or private law) or even as unrecognised associations, which is the most common situation in the case of Islam. Muslims have referred to the 1929 Act for the legal recognition of religious bodies only sporadically, partly because this "registration" implies an evaluation of statutes by the government and it is not always easy to obtain.[15]

1.4 Religious Communities as Associations

Religious communities, according to the freedoms enshrined in the Constitution, can organise themselves as associations or foundations, either with or without legal personality. Associations, foundations or other private entities may acquire legal personality under the terms of decree of the President of the Republic n. 361 of 2000 (which replaced the procedure previously established in Article 12 of the Civil Code); otherwise they can operate as unregistered

15 See above, note 33. Cf. Angelucci, Antonio, "L'associazionismo religioso musulmano tra diritto speciale e diritto comune: la centralità dello statuto", in Angelucci, Antonio, Bombardieri, Maria, and Tacchini, Davide (eds), *Islam e integrazione in Italia*, Venice: Marsilio, 2014, pp. 71–93.

associations, which are free to act and organise themselves in accordance with Article 36 of the Civil Code.

As has already been said, religious bodies recognised under Act n. 1159/1929 have a special status and they are entitled to some legal privileges; however, as the granting of this recognition can be complex, Muslim organisations often act as registered or unregistered associations. Among the most common legal structures of Muslim organisations we can find the voluntary association (o.d.v., organizzazione di volontariato) the non-profit-making organisation (ONLUS, *organizzazione non lucrativa di utilità sociale*) and the association with social purposes (a.p.s., *associazione di promozione sociale*). These types of organisations can obtain fiscal exemptions or similar advantages; however, associations with religious purposes may have problems when seeking to gain particular rights or legal treatment that Italian legislation normally grants to properly recognised religious bodies. For example, Muslim associations registered as "cultural associations" or a.p.s. have sometimes experienced difficulties with public authorities when asking for a building permit for a mosque.[16]

For these reasons, in some municipalities the competent administrative authorities are experimenting with new systems of relationships with local religious groups, creating a sort of catalogue in order to identify the associations with religious purposes. This is so for Milan, where municipal regulations have established a register of religious associations operating in the city area. This has the aim of listing all the associations with religious purposes, giving them a sort of "priority right" to contact the city authorities and to reach agreements granting specific rights (such as building permits for a place of worship). Any type of association can apply to be registered, as long as it has religious activities as its main aim, in accordance with the conditions established by a public announcement.[17] This possibility has been particularly used by Muslims, interested in acquiring a clearer and more transparent status.

Except for this case, there is usually no specific treatment for associations with religious purposes.

16 Floris, Pierangela, "Comunità islamiche e lacune normative. L'ente che non c'è: l'associazione con fine di religione e di culto".

17 See the website of the city of Milan: http://www.comune.milano.it/dseserver/webcity/GareContratti.nsf/weball/74437CB6254C94D7C1257ADA004D73B2?opendocument (last accessed 26 January 2015).

Codice civile
(Regio decreto 16 marzo 1942, n. 262: *Approvazione del testo del Codice civile*)
(GU n. 79 del 4-4-1942)[18]

Art. 36. *Ordinamento e amministrazione delle associazioni non riconosciute*
L'ordinamento interno e l'amministrazione delle associazioni non riconosciute come persone giuridiche sono regolati dagli accordi degli associati.
Le dette associazioni possono stare in giudizio nella persona di coloro ai quali, secondo questi accordi, è conferita la presidenza o la direzione.

D.P.R. 10 febbraio 2000, n. 361. *Regolamento recante norme per la semplificazione dei procedimenti di riconoscimento di persone giuridiche private e di approvazione delle modifiche dell'atto costitutivo e dello statuto (n. 17 dell'allegato 1 della legge 15 marzo 1997, n. 59)*[19]

Art. 1. *Procedimento per l'acquisto della personalità giuridica*
1. Salvo quanto previsto dagli articoli 7 e 9, le associazioni, le fondazioni e le altre istituzioni di carattere privato acquistano la personalità giuridica mediante il riconoscimento determinato dall'iscrizione nel registro delle persone giuridiche, istituito presso le prefetture.
2. La domanda per il riconoscimento di una persona giuridica, sottoscritta dal fondatore ovvero da coloro ai quali è conferita la rappresentanza dell'ente, è presentata alla prefettura nella cui provincia è stabilita la sede dell'ente. Alla domanda i richiedenti allegano copia autentica dell'atto costitutivo e dello statuto. La prefettura rilascia una ricevuta che attesta la data di presentazione della domanda.
3. Ai fini del riconoscimento è necessario che siano state soddisfatte le condizioni previste da norme di legge o di regolamento per la costituzione dell'ente, che lo scopo sia possibile e lecito e che il patrimonio risulti adeguato alla realizzazione dello scopo.
4. La consistenza del patrimonio deve essere dimostrata da idonea documentazione allegata alla domanda.

18 http://www.normattiva.it/uri-res/N2Ls?urn:nir:stato:regio.decreto:1942-03-16;262 (last accessed 26 January 2015).

19 www.normattiva.it/uri-res/N2Ls?urn:nir:stato:decreto.del.presidente.della.repubblica:2000-02-10;361 (last accessed 26 January 2015).

5. Entro il termine di centoventi giorni dalla data di presentazione della domanda il prefetto provvede all'iscrizione.
6. Qualora la prefettura ravvisi ragioni ostative all'iscrizione ovvero la necessità di integrare la documentazione presentata, entro il termine di cui al comma 5, ne dà motivata comunicazione ai richiedenti, i quali, nei successivi trenta giorni, possono presentare memorie e documenti. Se, nell'ulteriore termine di trenta giorni, il prefetto non comunica ai richiedenti il motivato diniego ovvero non provvede all'iscrizione, questa si intende negata.
7. Il riconoscimento delle fondazioni istituite per testamento può essere concesso dal prefetto, d'ufficio, in caso di ingiustificata inerzia del soggetto abilitato alla presentazione della domanda.
8. Le prefetture istituiscono il registro di cui al comma 1, entro novanta giorni dalla data di entrata in vigore del presente regolamento.
[...]

Art. 2. *Modificazioni dello statuto e dell'atto costitutivo*
1. Le modificazioni dello statuto e dell'atto costitutivo sono approvate con le modalità e nei termini previsti per l'acquisto della personalità giuridica dall'articolo 1, salvo i casi di riconoscimento della personalità giuridica per atto legislativo.
2. Alla domanda sono allegati i documenti idonei a dimostrare la sussistenza dei requisiti previsti dall'articolo 21, secondo comma, del codice civile.
3. Per le fondazioni, alla domanda è allegata la documentazione necessaria a comprovare il rispetto delle disposizioni statutarie inerenti al procedimento di modifica dello statuto.

Art. 3. *Registro delle persone giuridiche*
1. Il registro di cui all'articolo 1, comma 1, consta di due parti, l'una generale e l'altra analitica.
2. Nella prima parte del registro sono iscritte le persone giuridiche con la sola indicazione della loro denominazione.
3. L'iscrizione è contrassegnata da un numero d'ordine ed è accompagnata dall'indicazione della data, del nome del richiedente, delle pagine riservate nella parte analitica alla stessa persona giuridica e del volume in cui sono contenuti lo statuto e l'atto costitutivo e di quello dove sono raccolte le copie delle deliberazioni e dei provvedimenti iscritti nel registro. Alla fine della parte generale il registro è munito di una rubrica alfabetica contenente il nome della persona giuridica, il numero della pagina in cui la stessa è iscritta e il riferimento alla parte analitica del registro.
4. Nella seconda parte del registro, distintamente per ogni persona giuridica, sono iscritti tutti gli elementi e i fatti indicati nell'articolo 4.

[...]
8. Il registro e i documenti relativi possono essere esaminati da chiunque ne fa richiesta. La prefettura deve rilasciare gli estratti e i certificati che sono richiesti.
[...]

Art. 4. *Iscrizioni nel registro*
1. Nel registro devono essere indicati la data dell'atto costitutivo, la denominazione, lo scopo, il patrimonio, la durata, qualora sia stata determinata, la sede della persona giuridica e il cognome, il nome e il codice fiscale degli amministratori, con menzione di quelli ai quali è attribuita la rappresentanza.
2. Nel registro devono altresì essere iscritte le modificazioni dell'atto costitutivo e dello statuto, il trasferimento della sede e l'istituzione di sedi secondarie, la sostituzione degli amministratori, con indicazione di quelli ai quali è attribuita la rappresentanza, le deliberazioni di scioglimento, i provvedimenti che ordinano lo scioglimento o accertano l'estinzione, il cognome e nome dei liquidatori e tutti gli altri atti e fatti la cui iscrizione è espressamente prevista da norme di legge o di regolamento.

Art. 9. *Norme speciali*[20]
1. Le norme del presente regolamento sono applicabili ai procedimenti di riconoscimento delle associazioni previste dall'articolo 10 della legge 20 maggio 1985, n. 222, fatto salvo quanto disposto dal secondo e terzo comma del medesimo articolo.
2. Nulla è innovato nella disciplina degli enti ecclesiastici civilmente riconosciuti, in base alla legge 20 maggio 1985, n. 222, nonché degli enti civilmente riconosciuti in base alle leggi di approvazione di intese con le confessioni religiose ai sensi dell'articolo 8, terzo comma, della Costituzione. Nei confronti di tali enti trovano applicazione le disposizioni contenute negli articoli 3 e 4.

Legge n. 266 del 11 agosto 1991. *Legge Quadro sul volontariato*[21]

Art. 3.
Organizzazioni di volontariato

20 This Article refers to special rules about the legal personality of religious denominations that have signed an agreement with the state.

21 www.normattiva.it/uri-res/N2Ls?urn:nir:stato:legge:1991-08-11;266 (last accessed 26 January 2015).

1. È considerato organizzazione di volontariato ogni organismo liberamente costituito al fine di svolgere l'attività di cui all' art. 2, che si avvalga in modo determinante e prevalente delle prestazioni personali, volontarie e gratuite dei propri aderenti.
2. Le organizzazioni di volontariato possono assumere la forma giuridica che ritengono più adeguata al perseguimento dei loro fini, salvo il limite di compatibilità con lo scopo solidaristico.
3. Negli accordi degli aderenti, nell'atto costitutivo o nello statuto, oltre a quanto disposto dal codice civile per le diverse forme giuridiche che l'organizzazione assume, devono essere espressamente previsti l'assenza di fini di lucro, la democraticità della struttura, l'elettività e la gratuità delle cariche associative nonché la gratuità delle prestazioni fornite dagli aderenti, i criteri di ammissione e di esclusione di questi ultimi, i loro obblighi e diritti. Devono essere altresì stabiliti l'obbligo di formazione del bilancio, dal quale devono risultare i beni, i contributi o i lasciti ricevuti, nonché le modalità di approvazione dello stesso da parte dell'assemblea degli aderenti.
4. Le organizzazioni di volontariato possono assumere lavoratori dipendenti o avvalersi di prestazioni di lavoro autonomo esclusivamente nei limiti necessari al loro regolare funzionamento oppure occorrenti a qualificare e specializzare l'attività da essa svolta.
5. Le organizzazioni svolgono le attività di volontariato mediante strutture proprie o, nelle forme e nei modi previsti dalla legge, nell'ambito di strutture pubbliche o con queste convenzionate.

Decreto legislativo 4 dicembre 1997, n. 460. *Riordino della disciplina tributaria degli enti non commerciali e delle organizzazioni non lucrative di utilità sociale* (*ONLUS*)[22]

Art. 10—Organizzazioni non lucrative di utilità sociale[23]

1. Sono organizzazioni non lucrative di utilità sociale (ONLUS) le associazioni, i comitati, le fondazioni, le società cooperative e gli altri enti di carattere

22 www.normattiva.it/uri-res/N2Ls?urn:nir:stato:decreto.legislativo:1997-12-04;460 (last accessed 26 January 2015).

23 Article 10 is about the institution of Organisations without economic purposes (ONLUS) and their characteristics; other Articles of the decree (art. 12, 14, 17, 18, 19, 20, 21, 22, 23, 24) introduced changes (rebates and exemptions) in different tax laws, in favour of ONLUS. On economic support of religious denominations and associations with religious purposes see chapter 3.

privato, con o senza personalità giuridica, i cui statuti o atti costitutivi, redatti nella forma dell'atto pubblico o della scrittura privata autenticata o registrata, prevedono espressamente:
a) lo svolgimento di attività in uno o più dei seguenti settori:
1) assistenza sociale e socio-sanitaria;
2) assistenza sanitaria;
3) beneficenza;
4) istruzione;
5) formazione;
6) sport dilettantistico;
7) tutela, promozione e valorizzazione delle cose d'interesse artistico e storico di cui alla legge 1 giugno 1939, n. 1089, ivi comprese le biblioteche e i beni di cui al decreto del Presidente della Repubblica 30 settembre 1963, n. 1409;
8) tutela e valorizzazione della natura e dell'ambiente, con esclusione dell'attività, esercitata abitualmente, di raccolta e riciclaggio dei rifiuti urbani, speciali e pericolosi di cui all'articolo 7 del decreto legislativo 5 febbraio 1997, n. 22;
9) promozione della cultura e dell'arte;
10) tutela dei diritti civili;
11) ricerca scientifica di particolare interesse sociale svolta direttamente da fondazioni ovvero da esse affidata ad università, enti di ricerca ed altre fondazioni che la svolgono direttamente, in ambiti e secondo modalità da definire con apposito regolamento governativo emanato ai sensi dell'articolo 17 della legge 23 agosto 1988, n. 400;
b) l'esclusivo perseguimento di finalità di solidarietà sociale;
c) il divieto di svolgere attività diverse da quelle menzionate alla lettera a) ad eccezione di quelle ad esse direttamente connesse;
d) il divieto di distribuire, anche in modo indiretto, utili e avanzi di gestione nonché fondi, riserve o capitale durante la vita dell'organizzazione, a meno che la destinazione o la distribuzione non siano imposte per legge o siano effettuate a favore di altre ONLUS che per legge, statuto o regolamento fanno parte della medesima ed unitaria struttura;
e) l'obbligo di impiegare gli utili o gli avanzi di gestione per la realizzazione delle attività istituzionali e di quelle ad esse direttamente connesse;
f) l'obbligo di devolvere il patrimonio dell'organizzazione, in caso di suo scioglimento per qualunque causa, ad altre organizzazioni non lucrative di utilità sociale o a fini di pubblica utilità, sentito l'organismo di controllo di cui all'articolo 3, comma 190, della legge 23 dicembre 1996, n. 662, salvo diversa destinazione imposta dalla legge;
g) l'obbligo di redigere il bilancio o rendiconto annuale;

h) disciplina uniforme del rapporto associativo e delle modalità associative volte a garantire l'effettività del rapporto medesimo, escludendo espressamente la temporaneità della partecipazione alla vita associativa e prevedendo per gli associati o partecipanti maggiori d'età il diritto di voto per l'approvazione e le modificazioni dello statuto e dei regolamenti e per la nomina degli organi direttivi dell'associazione;
i) l'uso, nella denominazione ed in qualsivoglia segno distintivo o comunicazione rivolta al pubblico, della locuzione "organizzazione non lucrativa di utilità sociale" o dell'acronimo
"ONLUS".
[...]

Art. 11. *Anagrafe delle ONLUS e decadenza dalle agevolazioni*
1. E' istituita presso il Ministero delle finanze l'anagrafe unica delle ONLUS.
[...]

Legge 7 dicembre 2000, n. 383. Disciplina delle associazioni di promozione sociale.
(GU n. 300 del 27-12-2000)[24]

Art. 1. *Finalità e oggetto della legge*
1. La Repubblica riconosce il valore sociale dell'associazionismo liberamente costituito e delle sue molteplici attività come espressione di partecipazione, solidarietà e pluralismo; ne promuove lo sviluppo in tutte le sue articolazioni territoriali, nella salvaguardia della sua autonomia; favorisce il suo apporto originale al conseguimento di finalità di carattere sociale, civile, culturale e di ricerca etica e spirituale.
2. La presente legge, in attuazione degli articoli 2, 3, secondo comma, 4, secondo comma, 9 e 18 della Costituzione, detta principi fondamentali e norme per la valorizzazione dell'associazionismo di promozione sociale e stabilisce i principi cui le regioni e le province autonome devono attenersi nel disciplinare i rapporti fra le istituzioni pubbliche e le associazioni di promozione sociale nonché i criteri cui debbono uniformarsi le amministrazioni statali e gli enti locali nei medesimi rapporti.
3. La presente legge ha, altresì, lo scopo di favorire il formarsi di nuove realtà associative e di consolidare e rafforzare quelle già esistenti che rispondono agli obiettivi di cui al presente articolo.

24 www.normattiva.it/uri-res/N2Ls?urn:nir:stato:legge:2000-12-07;383 (last access 26 January 2015).

Art. 2. *Associazioni di promozione sociale*

1. Sono considerate associazioni di promozione sociale le associazioni riconosciute e non riconosciute, i movimenti, i gruppi e i loro coordinamenti o federazioni costituiti al fine di svolgere attività di utilità sociale a favore di associati o di terzi, senza finalità di lucro e nel pieno rispetto della libertà e dignità degli associati.

2. Non sono considerate associazioni di promozione sociale, ai fini e per gli effetti della presente legge, i partiti politici, le organizzazioni sindacali, le associazioni dei datori di lavoro, le associazioni professionali e di categoria e tutte le associazioni che hanno come finalità la tutela esclusiva di interessi economici degli associati.

3. Non costituiscono altresì associazioni di promozione sociale i circoli privati e le associazioni comunque denominate che dispongono limitazioni con riferimento alle condizioni economiche e discriminazioni di qualsiasi natura in relazione all'ammissione degli associati o prevedono il diritto di trasferimento, a qualsiasi titolo, della quota associativa o che, infine, collegano, in qualsiasi forma, la partecipazione sociale alla titolarità di azioni o quote di natura patrimoniale.

Art. 3. *Atto costitutivo e statuto*

1. Le associazioni di promozione sociale si costituiscono con atto scritto nel quale deve tra l'altro essere indicata la sede legale. Nello statuto devono essere espressamente previsti:

a) la denominazione;
b) l'oggetto sociale;
c) l'attribuzione della rappresentanza legale dell'associazione;
d) l'assenza di fini di lucro e la previsione che i proventi delle attività non possono, in nessun caso, essere divisi fra gli associati, anche in forme indirette;
e) l'obbligo di reinvestire l'eventuale avanzo di gestione a favore di attività istituzionali statutariamente previste;
f) le norme sull'ordinamento interno ispirato a principi di democrazia e di uguaglianza dei diritti di tutti gli associati, con la previsione dell'elettività delle cariche associative. In relazione alla particolare natura di talune associazioni, il Ministro per la solidarietà sociale, sentito l'Osservatorio nazionale di cui all'articolo 11, può consentire deroghe alla presente disposizione;
g) i criteri per l'ammissione e l'esclusione degli associati ed i loro diritti e obblighi;
h) l'obbligo di redazione di rendiconti economico-finanziari, nonché le modalità di approvazione degli stessi da parte degli organi statutari;
i) le modalità di scioglimento dell'associazione;

l) l'obbligo di devoluzione del patrimonio residuo in caso di scioglimento, cessazione o estinzione, dopo la liquidazione, a fini di utilità sociale.

Art. 6. *Rappresentanza*
1. Le associazioni di promozione sociale anche non riconosciute sono rappresentate in giudizio dai soggetti ai quali, secondo lo statuto, è conferita la rappresentanza legale.
2. Per le obbligazioni assunte dalle persone che rappresentano l'associazione di promozione sociale i terzi creditori devono far valere i loro diritti sul patrimonio dell'associazione medesima e, solo in via sussidiaria, possono rivalersi nei confronti delle persone che hanno agito in nome e per conto dell'associazione.

Art. 7. *Registri*
1. Presso la Presidenza del Consiglio dei Ministri—Dipartimento per gli affari sociali è istituito un registro nazionale al quale possono iscriversi, ai fini dell'applicazione della presente legge, le associazioni di promozione sociale a carattere nazionale in possesso dei requisiti di cui all'articolo 2, costituite ed operanti da almeno un anno. Alla tenuta del registro si provvede con le ordinarie risorse finanziarie, umane e strumentali del Dipartimento per gli affari sociali.
[...]
4. Le regioni e le province autonome di Trento e di Bolzano istituiscono, rispettivamente, registri su scala regionale e provinciale, cui possono iscriversi tutte le associazioni in possesso dei requisiti di cui all'articolo 2, che svolgono attività, rispettivamente, in ambito regionale o provinciale.

Comune di Milano. Deliberazione della Giunta 6 luglio 2012, n. 1444. ***Approvazione delle linee di indirizzo per la promozione del dialogo interreligioso e per il sostegno del diritto della libertà di culto delle comunità religiose presenti sul territorio cittadino***[25]

La giunta comunale
premesso che:
La Carta Costituzionale sancisce il diritto di professare le proprie convinzioni anche religiose. In particolare:

25 Published in *Quaderni di diritto e politica ecclesiastica*, 2013, n. 2, 540–542.

– l'art. 3 prevede la non discriminazione in base a ragioni legate al sesso, alla razza, alla lingua alle opinioni politiche, alle condizioni personali e sociali e alla religione assegnando allo Stato il compito di rimuovere gli ostacoli di ordine economico e sociale che, limitando di fatto la libertà dei cittadini, impediscono il pieno sviluppo della persona umana e l'effettiva partecipazione all'organizzazione politica, economica e sociale del paese;
– gli artt. 18 e 21 riconoscono per tutti il diritto di associazione e di manifestare il proprio pensiero;
– gli arti. 8, 19 e 20 riconoscono a «tutti», individui e gruppi, in condizioni di uguale libertà, il diritto di libertà religiosa quale espressione fondamentale della persona nonché il diritto delle confessioni religiose di potersi organizzare autonomamente secondo propri statuti.
La tutela della libera espressione religiosa costituisce, pertanto, uno dei cardini più importanti delle democrazie costituzionali contemporanee. Tale principio, del resto, è fortemente radicato nell'ordinamento internazionale quale sommo bene della persona umana, il cui godimento non può subire restrizioni per effetto di fattori quali la condizione economica, la razza, la cittadinanza, il sesso, ecc.;
– Va inoltre ricordato che, con il riconoscimento del principio supremo della laicità dello Stato, la Corte costituzionale ha inserito il diritto di libertà religiosa all'interno di un orizzonte di pluralismo culturale e religioso in cui tutti gli attori sociali, ivi inclusi quelli religiosamente connotati, sono chiamati a dare il loro contributo alla costruzione del «bene comune» ovvero, traslando tale concetto sul piano locale, alla «città comune»;
– In applicazione del dettato costituzionale le pubbliche istituzioni sono chiamate a facilitare e sostenere il libero esercizio dei culti, dovere che diviene vero e proprio obbligo a rimuovere gli ostacoli che potrebbero comprometterne l'esercizio;
– Le caratteristiche odierne assunte dal tessuto sociale cittadino, caratterizzato dalla presenza di numerose comunità dalla più varia provenienza, pone alla città l'urgenza di avviare un dialogo costante e continuo con le diverse appartenenze religiose, facendo della diversità una risorsa positiva dello sviluppo sociale;
– Si rende pertanto necessario rimediare ad una situazione di totale assenza dell'Amministrazione comunale rispetto ad un fenomeno significativo che chiede di essere riconosciuto, governato e ricondotto all'interno di un «patto» che identifichi e riconosca i diritti e doveri di tutte le parti coinvolte;
– Il Comune, pertanto, nell'ambito delle proprie competenze e in ottemperanza al dettato costituzionale, nella convinzione che un rapporto attento con e tra le comunità religiose costituisca un fattore importante per la costruzione

di una pacifica e civile convivenza, intende sviluppare un dialogo aperto, trasparente e regolare con tutte le realtà attive nel proprio ambito territoriale al fine di condividere e costruire un sentimento comune di responsabilità nel confronti della città;
– Il Comune, di conseguenza, si impegna a rendere operative tutte le proprie competenze in materia di diritto di libertà religiosa nella convinzione che il pieno godimento di tale diritto costituisca un tassello fondamentale nella costruzione di una cittadinanza condivisa;
– Tale volontà è stata inoltre recepita all'interno del «Piano Generale di Sviluppo 2011–2016» approvato dal Consiglio Comunale con deliberazione n. 9 del 12.03.2012, con cui si ribadiva la necessità di operare per il riconoscimento della libertà religiosa quale impegno per la costruzione di una città coesa capace di sviluppare partecipazione e inclusione sociale;

rilevato che:
– Si è inteso avviare un più attivo e stretto confronto con il «Forum delle Religioni», costituitosi nel 2004 sulla base dell'invito che l'Arcidiocesi milanese aveva rivolto ad ogni comunità e organizzazione religiosa presente a Milano, al fine di sviluppare una reciproca conoscenza nel rispetto della diversità dei culti e in una logica di pacifica, cordiale e rispettosa convivenza sul territorio cittadino;
– Si è proceduto a costituire un «Gruppo di lavoro per il Dialogo Interreligioso» composto da esperti nelle discipline legate alle tematiche religiose che hanno collaborato e collaborano, a titolo volontario, con l'Amministrazione Comunale per identificare le problematiche più significative legate al diritto di libertà religiosa e promuovere iniziative di scambio, confronto e collaborazione tra le diverse organizzazioni e associazioni presenti in città;
– il gruppo di lavoro ha incontrato i referenti delle singole realtà confessionali e, in particolare, ha attuato una ricognizione dei luoghi in cui viene esercitato il culto, elaborando una mappa dell'esistente e avviando un colloquio con tutte le comunità attive nell'area cittadina con l'obiettivo di giungere ad accordi condivisi per un esercizio ordinato del culto, da svilupparsi non ai margini del diritto ma in armonia con la vita cittadina nel suo insieme e in conformità alle normative vigenti;
– il dialogo avviato è stato molto positivo e ha permesso di rilevare la necessità di promuovere un «tavolo permanente di confronto» con le realtà confessionali sia per affrontare specifiche problematiche relative ai singoli gruppi sia per sviluppare il confronto e promuovere azioni positive e partecipate sul territorio;

– tra le tematiche più significative emerse negli incontri, già realizzati dal Gruppo di lavoro con le diverse comunità vi è la necessità di disporre di luoghi idonei in cui poter praticare pubblicamente il culto in condizioni dignitose;
– tale necessità è una facoltà coessenziale al diritto di libertà religiosa e pertanto, per un consolidato orientamento della giurisprudenza costituzionale, non riservata alle sole confessioni religiose che abbiano stipulato un'intesa con lo Stato ma fruibili da parte di tutti i gruppi religiosi presenti sul territorio cittadino.
considerato che:
– si rende necessario definire criteri e modalità per assicurare lo svolgimento del culto pubblico, da praticare nel rispetto delle regole di civile convivenza, evitando atteggiamenti di emarginazione di un diritto sancito costituzionalmente;
– per poter garantire tale diritto si ritiene essenziale identificare preliminarmente i criteri che, in conformità alla legislazione vigente, dovranno caratterizzare i soggetti confessionali abilitati a fruire della destinazione d'uso per fini cultuali di spazi di proprietà sia pubblica sia privata;
– successivamente si dovrà procedere all'indizione di un Avviso pubblico per la costituzione di uno speciale «Albo» delle organizzazioni e/o associazioni che, in possesso dei requisiti richiesti, potranno richiedere la messa a norma degli spazi in uso per l'esercizio del culto e/o beneficiare della destinazione di aree e/o spazi pubblici e/o privati per lo svolgimento di attività riconducibili alla pratica pubblica del proprio culto;
– le organizzazioni e/o associazioni di cui all'Albo, al momento della loro iscrizione, si impegnano a sottoscrivere un Protocollo d'impegno con l'Amministrazione Comunale in cui saranno declinati i diritti e i doveri delle parti al fine di garantire un ordinato svolgimento del culto nel rispetto dell'ordinamento giuridico italiano e della civile convivenza, nonché la realizzazione di momenti di incontro, dialogo e confronto;
– effettuata l'iscrizione e ratificato il Protocollo i soggetti abilitati potranno presentare istanza al Comune per ottenere le autorizzazioni necessarie alla messa a norma degli spazi già in uso o per partecipare a procedure pubbliche per la destinazione di nuove aree o strutture destinate all'esercizio del culto;
– le comunità religiose iscritte all'Albo, invitate a dare il proprio contributo alle iniziative di dialogo interculturale e interreligioso, saranno chiamate a partecipare alla costituzione di una «Conferenza permanente delle Confessioni Religiose» che, promossa dall'amministrazione comunale, permetterà di sviluppare una più approfondita conoscenza delle e tra le realtà con-

fessionali, il monitoraggio e la soluzione delle eventuali criticità rilevate e l'attivazione di iniziative e attività di incontro rivolte alla popolazione cittadina,
– per poter dare attuazione al percorso sopra descritto si rende opportuno provvedere alla nomina di una Commissione di esperti in grado di:
1. Individuare i criteri e i requisiti da inserire nell'Avviso pubblico per l'identificazione dei soggetti confessionali abilitati all'iscrizione all'«Albo delle Organizzazioni e delle Associazioni Religiose»;
2. Definire il testo del Protocollo tra il Comune di Milano e le organizzazioni/associazioni di cui al precedente Albo finalizzato al corretto svolgimento delle attività legate all'esercizio pubblico del culto e alla promozione di iniziative per la reciproca conoscenza degli specifici patrimoni spirituali;
– Per l'attuazione delle funzioni e compiti sopra descritti la Commissione sopra citata, da nominarsi con provvedimento sindacale, dovrà essere composta da studiosi ed esperti nelle diverse confessioni religiose e di diritto delle religioni ed eventualmente integrata da dirigenti/funzionari dell'Amministrazione Comunale;
– Con successivi provvedimenti si procederà all'approvazione dei lavori della Commissione e alla definizione delle modalità di individuazione delle nuove aree e/o strutture pubbliche e/o private da destinare al culto;
– Le aree o strutture pubbliche identificate saranno assegnate attraverso procedure ad evidenza pubblica;

atteso che:
– Sussistono gli estremi di urgenza, in considerazione della necessità di avviare le azioni necessarie a assicurare la libertà dell'esercizio del culto nel rispetto delle normative vigenti e delle regole di civile convivenza, se ne propone l'immediata eseguibilità;

visti
– Gli art. 3,8, 19, 20 e 21 della Costituzione italiana;
– gli artt. 48, 49 e 134 4° comma del Decreto Legislativo n. 267 del 18 agosto 2000;
– La Deliberazione di Consiglio Comunale n. 9 del 12.03.2012;
– il parere di regolarità tecnica espresso, ai sensi dell'art. 49 del Decreto Legislativo 18 agosto 2000, n. 267, dal Direttore di Settore competente allegato quale parte integrante al presente provvedimento;
– il parere di legittimità espresso dal Segretario Generale, allegato quale parte integrante al presente provvedimento;

delibera
– di approvare le linee di indirizzo per la promozione del dialogo interreligioso e per il sostegno del diritto della libertà di culto delle comunità religiose presenti sul territorio cittadino descritte in premessa;
– di dare atto che con provvedimento sindacale si procederà all'individuazione e nomina dei componenti la Commissione per l'attuazione delle attività specificate in premessa;
– di dare atto che con successivi provvedimenti si procederà all'approvazione dei lavori della Commissione e alla definizione delle modalità di individuazione delle nuove aree e/o strutture pubbliche e/o private da destinare al culto;
– di dare atto che le aree o strutture pubbliche identificate saranno assegnate attraverso procedure ad evidenza pubblica.

Comune di Milano. Deliberazione della Giunta 30 novembre 2012, n. 2475. *Approvazione degli indirizzi e dei criteri per l'iscrizione in un albo delle associazioni e organizzazioni religiose presenti sul territorio cittadino*[26]

La giunta comunale
premesso che:
La Carta Costituzionale, integrando il principio supremo di laicità dello Stato, sancisce agli artt. 2, 3, 7, 8, 19 e 20 il diritto a professare le proprie convinzioni religiose, a manifestare il proprio pensiero e credo religioso nonché il diritto a poter esercitare il culto relativo all'ambito religioso di appartenenza;
la tutela della libera espressione religiosa costituisce un diritto fondamentale della persona umana, che non può e non deve subire restrizioni per effetto di fattori quali la condizione economica, la razza, la cittadinanza, il sesso, ecc.;
in applicazione del dettato costituzionale le pubbliche istituzioni sono chiamate a facilitare e sostenere la libera manifestazione del culto, dovere che diviene vero e proprio obbligo a rimuovere gli ostacoli che potrebbero comprometterne l'esercizio quale facoltà essenziale del diritto costituzionale di libertà religiosa;
le caratteristiche odierne assunte dal tessuto sociale cittadino, caratterizzato dalla presenza di numerose comunità dalla più varia provenienza, hanno posto all'Amministrazione Comunale l'urgenza di avviare un dialogo costante e continuo con le diverse appartenenze religiose, nella convinzione che un rapporto attento con e tra le comunità costituisca un fattore importante per

26 Published in *Quaderni di diritto e politica ecclesiastica*, 2013, n. 2, 590–593.

la costruzione di una pacifica e civile convivenza, in cui la diversità, anche religiosa, può divenire una risorsa positiva per lo sviluppo sociale;
tale consapevolezza è stata ribadita all'interno del «Piano generale di Sviluppo del Comune di Milano 2011–2016» che ha posto il tema del sostegno e della tutela del diritto di libertà religiosa tra gli obiettivi trasversali in grado di garantire uno sviluppo coeso e partecipe del contesto sociale;
la Giunta Comunale, in ottemperanza al dettato costituzionale e nell'ambito delle proprie competenze, con deliberazione n. 1444 del 06/07/2012 ha approvato le linee di indirizzo per la promozione del dialogo interreligioso e il sostegno al diritto della libertà di culto per tutte le comunità religiose presenti sul territorio cittadino;
nel provvedimento sopra citato, al fine di avviare un positivo dialogo con le realtà cultuali per la costruzione di una pacifica e civile convivenza, si prevedeva l'indizione di un Avviso pubblico per la costituzione di uno speciale «Albo» delle Associazioni/Organizzazioni Religiose e l'elaborazione di un «Protocollo» di reciproco impegno per la promozione del dialogo tra le diverse appartenenze religiose e il libero esercizio del culto nel rispetto dell'ordinamento giuridico vigente;
nella stessa deliberazione la Giunta Comunale ha altresì previsto la costituzione di una Commissione di Esperti, da nominarsi con provvedimento sindacale, con il compito di:
– Individuare i criteri e i requisiti da inserire nell'Avviso pubblico per l'identificazione dei soggetti confessionali abilitati all'iscrizione all' «Albo delle Associazioni e delle Organizzazioni Religiose»;
– Definire il testo del Protocollo tra il Comune di Milano e le Organizzazioni/Associazioni richiedenti l'iscrizione all'Albo;
– con provvedimento sindacale del 25.07.2012 Atti PG.n. 489263/2012 è stata costituita la Commissione di Esperti composta da docenti universitari con pluriennale esperienza nel campo del diritto canonico ed ecclesiastico e del diritto comparato delle religioni;

considerato che:
– la Commissione si è periodicamente riunita, come da verbali conservati agli atti, per approfondire le tematiche riguardanti i compiti ad essa affidati ed elaborare una proposta che nel rispetto del dettato costituzionale e delle norme nazionali e regionali, sia in grado di garantire lo sviluppo del dialogo interreligioso e il sostegno alla libera espressione del culto;
– le caratteristiche assunte dall'Albo e criteri e i requisiti da inserire nell'Avviso pubblico identificati dalla Commissione sono sinteticamente così articolati:

– L'Albo
L'Albo delle Associazioni/Organizzazioni religiose, nel rispetto dei principi sanciti dalla Costituzione in merito alla tutela del diritto di libertà religiosa, avrà una «natura dichiarativa» e l'iscrizione allo stesso avverrà esclusivamente previo accertamento della corretta presentazione della documentazione richiesta e della sussistenza dei requisiti previsti dall'Avviso pubblico e attestanti il carattere religioso dell'attività svolta dalle associazioni e/o organizzazioni richiedenti;
l'iscrizione all'Albo sarà accessibile da parte di tutte le Associazioni/Organizzazioni dal cui statuto risulti l'esclusività o, almeno, la chiara prevalenza di attività legate alla pratica cultuale e religiosa. Il perseguimento esclusivo e/o prevalente del fine di religione o di culto costituisce requisito essenziale per l'iscrizione all'Albo. L'Albo non riguarderà quindi le realtà associative, anche religiosamente orientate, con finalità non immediatamente dirette alla pratica religiosa.
L'iscrizione, condizionata dalla presenza dei requisiti richiesti, avrà lo scopo di fornire al Comune un valido supporto per l'esecuzione delle disposizioni previste dalla Legge Regionale n. 12 del 2005 in materia di culto. L'iscrizione all'Albo potrà, inoltre, costituire un elemento di facilitazione per la partecipazione a procedure pubbliche per la destinazione di strutture e/o aree demaniali per servizi religiosi, in quanto le associazioni risulteranno già in possesso del requisito della «confessionalità» richiesto dall'art. 70 della citata legge regionale.
L'Albo, per la sua natura aperta, potrà altresì costituire uno strumento utile per i Settori del Comune di Milano che si trovino ad occuparsi, a vario titolo, di associazionismo religioso e libero esercizio del culto.

– Requisiti e documentazione
Ai fini dell'iscrizione all'Albo le associazioni/organizzazioni religiose dovranno presentare:
1. Copia dell'Atto costitutivo e dello Statuto dell'associazione e/o organizzazione da cui risultino: il carattere religioso esclusivo e/o prevalente, finalità ed attività svolte; organi direttivi e meccanismi deliberativi interni, nel rispetto dell'ordinamento italiano;
2. dichiarazione a firma del legale rappresentante riportante le seguenti informazioni:
a. indicazione della specifica tradizione religiosa di appartenenza del gruppo;
b. indicazioni di eventuali affiliazioni con altre associazioni, enti e/o organizzazioni pubblici o privati;
c. descrizione delle attività svolte dalla costituzione dell'associazione e/o organizzazione e delle attività attualmente in essere;

d. indicazione della/e sede/i;
e. indicazione dei soggetti che ricoprono cariche direttive all'interno dell'associazione e/o organizzazione all'atto della domanda e, tra questi ultimi, un referente responsabile per eventuali comunicazioni;
f. impegno alla tempestiva comunicazione delle variazioni delle informazioni fornite e alla loro eventuale integrazione.
La Commissione, nel rispetto del dettato costituzionale in tema di diritto alla libera espressione religiosa, ha ritenuto che il «Protocollo» debba assumere le caratteristiche di un «documento ricapitolativo» delle norme e delle regole già vigenti nell'ordinamento in materia di esercizio del culto nel rispetto della civile convivenza. Per questa sua caratteristica, il testo del Protocollo dovrà essere allegato all'istanza di richiesta di inserimento nell'Albo e siglato dal Legale rappresentante dell'associazione/organizzazione richiedente quale «presa d'atto» di quanto in esso riportato. Con la restituzione del Protocollo, allegato alla domanda di iscrizione all'Albo, l'Associazione o Organizzazione richiedente dà atto di aver preso visione di tale Protocollo e manifesta l'impegno di rispettarne i contenuti, così da stabilire con la Città un dialogo aperto e trasparente.
[...]

delibera
di approvare gli indirizzi e i criteri individuati dalla Commissione di Esperti e descritti in premessa, per l'iscrizione ad un «Albo delle Associazioni e Organizzazioni Religiose» presenti sul territorio cittadino;
di approvare i contenuti essenziali del Protocollo di cui al documento sub 1) allegato quale parte integrante alla presente deliberazione;
di incaricare il Direttore competente a presidiare e coordinare gli aspetti amministrativi connessi ai rapporti con le Comunità religiose ad adottare tutti gli atti conseguenti e necessari nel rispetto degli indirizzi e criteri sopra citati;
di dare atto che si provvederà all'aggiornamento annuale dell'Albo e che, in considerazione dell'innovatività della procedura avviata, per l'anno 2013 si procederà un aggiornamento semestrale dello stesso a partire dalla data della sua approvazione.

1.5 Ministers of Religion (Recognition)

Article 3 of Act n. 1159/1929 is about the recognition of ministers of the "admitted cults". It is for the religious denominations to appoint someone as minister of religion; the appointment shall be approved and recognised by the state if the ministers wish to perform some acts with civil effects (for example to celebrate a religious marriage with civil effects). However, recognition is not a necessary condition for acting in Italy. Conditions for obtaining recognition are set out in Royal decree n. 289 of 1930: the minister of religion must submit a request to the Minister of the Interior, who will check that the claimant meets certain criteria. In particular, the request shall document the religious act of the appointment as a minister of worship, showing that the appointment was made in accordance with the religious rules of the denomination (Art. 20 of the royal decree of 1930). Moreover, if the religious minister will be in charge of celebrating religious marriages with civil effects, the Ministry of the Interior shall approve his appointment only if he is an Italian citizen and can demonstrate competence in knowledge of Italian (Articles 21–22 of the Royal decree). The recognition of a minister of religion is also necessary to be admitted as a chaplain in the armed forces (Article 8 of Royal decree n. 289/1930) and, broadly speaking, for all acts that have civil effects. Otherwise, other rights and functions can be freely performed by the ministers of all religions.

Here it is worth noting that the 1929–1930 provisions regulating the recognition of religious ministers have never been applied to Islam. This is due to the fact that Italian legislation is shaped on the model of Catholic (or Christian) churches and Islamic imams barely fit into the category (there is no specific act of appointment of imams, who are often simply the guides in the prayers; rules on how the appointment is made are not fixed in a written regulation, etc.).[27] Even if Islamic law does not provide for a category of proper "ministers" (in the Christian sense of the word), it is important to remember that the notion of "religious minister" is used by the Italian State "to indicate a legal status that is attributed to those persons who … plays a different role in respect to other 'normal' believers".[28] Therefore, the specific tasks of

27 See introduction and Chapter 1; see Carnì, Matteo, "Islam e ministri di culto", in Cardia, Carlo and Dalla Torre, Giuseppe, *Comunità islamiche in Italia. Identità e forme giuridiche*, pp. 211–243.

28 Alicino, Francesco, "Imams and other Religious Authorities in Italy", in "Stato Chiese e Pluralismo Confessionale", online journal, n. 1 of 12 January 2015 (at http://www.statoechiese.it/images/stories/2015.1/alicino.m2_imams.pdf).

imams might be a starting point for their appointment as ministers of the Islamic religion.

Legge 24 giugno 1929 n. 1159. ***Disposizioni sull'esercizio dei culti ammessi nello Stato e sul matrimonio celebrato davanti ai ministri dei culti medesimi***

Art. 3
Le nomine dei ministri dei culti diversi dalla religione dello Stato debbono essere notificate al Ministero dell'Interno per l'approvazione. Nessun effetto civile può essere riconosciuto agli atti del proprio ministero compiuti da tali ministri di culto, se la loro nomina non abbia ottenuto l'approvazione governativa.

Regio Decreto 28 febbraio 1930, n. 289. ***Norme per l'attuazione della legge 24 giugno 1929, n. 1159/1929, sui culti ammessi nello Stato e per il coordinamento di essa con le altre leggi dello Stato***

Art. 3
I ministri di un culto ammesso nello stato, la nomina dei quali sia stata approvata a termini dell'art. 3 della legge, possono pubblicare ed affiggere nell'interno ed alle porte esterne degli edifici destinati al proprio culto gli atti riguardanti il governo spirituale dei fedeli, senza particolare licenza dell'autorità di pubblica sicurezza e con esenzione da tasse.
Tali atti debbono essere scritti in lingua italiana, salva la facoltà di aggiungere, accanto al testo italiano, la traduzione in altre lingue.

Art. 4
I ministri di un culto ammesso nel stato, la nomina dei quali sia stata approvata a termini dell'art. 3 della legge, possono, senza alcuna ingerenza delle autorità civili, eseguire collette nell'interno ed all'ingresso degli edifici destinati al proprio culto.

Art. 5
I ministri dei culti ammessi nel stato possono essere autorizzati a frequentare i luoghi di cura e di ritiro per prestare l'assistenza religiosa ai ricoverati che la domandino.
L'autorizzazione è data da chi è preposto alla direzione amministrativa del luogo di cura o di ritiro e deve indicare le modalità o le cautele con cui l'assistenza deve essere prestata.

Art. 6
I ministri dei culti ammessi nel stato possono essere autorizzati a prestare l'assistenza religiosa agli internati negli istituti di prevenzione e di pena, ogni qualvolta ne siano richiesti dagli internati stessi o dai familiari o da chi abbia la tutela giuridica dei medesimi, sotto l'osservanza delle norme contenute nei regolamenti speciali per detti istituti.

Art. 7
In caso di mobilitazione delle forze armate dello Stato, i ministri di un culto ammesso nel regno, la nomina dei quali sia stata approvata a termini dell'art. 3 della legge, possono essere dispensati dalla chiamata alle armi su attestazione del Prefetto, il quale dichiari che l'opera loro è assolutamente indispensabile e insostituibile per l'assistenza religiosa dei fedeli affidati alle loro cure.

Art. 8
In caso di mobilitazione delle forze armate dello Stato, l'assistenza religiosa dei militari acattolici, da esercitarsi da ministri di un culto ammesso nel regno la nomina dei quali sia stata approvata a termini dell'art. 3 della legge, può essere autorizzata dall'autorità militare cui è stata affidata la suprema direzione delle operazioni belliche.
Alla stessa autorità spetta di stabilire le norme e le cautele con le quali tale assistenza può essere esercitata.

Art. 20
L'approvazione delle nomine dei ministri di culto, di cui all'art. 3 della legge, è chiesta con domanda diretta al Ministro dell'Interno, dal ministro di culto interessato.
La domanda è presentata all'ufficio per gli affari di culto presso la prefettura, e deve essere corredata dell'atto, in originale od in copia autentica, di nomina, dei documenti atti a provare che la nomina stessa è avvenuta secondo le norme che regolano il culto cui il ministro appartiene.
Qualora il culto non sia, o per erezione dei suoi istituti in ente morale od altrimenti, già noto al governo, debbono essere fornite anche notizie circa la denominazione di esso, i suoi scopi, i suoi riti, i mezzi finanziari dei quali dispone, i nomi degli amministratori, l'autorità ecclesiastica superiore da cui dipende.

Art. 21
Gli uffici per gli affari di culto, assunte le altre informazioni necessarie per completare l'istruttoria e sentito il Prefetto della provincia in cui il ministro del culto esercita il suo ufficio, trasmettono gli atti al Ministero dell'Interno.
L'approvazione della nomina è data con decreto del Ministro dell'Interno.

Nel caso in cui i seguaci del culto, cui appartiene il ministro di culto che chiede l'approvazione della propria nomina, siano nella maggioranza cittadini italiani oppure nel caso in cui al ministro del culto spetti la facoltà di celebrare matrimoni religiosi dei propri fedeli con effetti civili, a termini dell'art. 7 della legge, il ministro del culto deve avere la cittadinanza italiana e saper parlare la lingua italiana.

Art. 22
Copia del decreto ministeriale di approvazione della nomina dei ministri di culto è comunicata agli uffici per gli affari di culto presso le prefetture, i quali ne trasmettono immediatamente copia all'ufficio dello stato civile del comune in cui il ministro del culto ha la propria residenza per ragione del proprio ufficio.
Gli atti del proprio ministero compiuti dai ministri di culto sono operativi agli effetti civili dalla data del decreto ministeriale di approvazione della nomina dei ministri medesimi.

CHAPTER 2

Relations between the State and Islam

2.1 Introduction

As seen before (chapter 1), Articles 7 and 8 of the Italian Constitution state that relations between the state and religious denominations are governed by bilateral agreements; non-Catholic confessions can sign separate accords (*intese*) with the government in accordance with Article 8.3. Islam, like other confessions, has not signed an agreement with the state, so it is subject to the legislation of 1929 (see above, section 1). Among the problems that have hindered the community's efforts to sign an accord we can find the division of the Italian Islamic community, organised in multiple and different groups, often without relations or cooperation among them.[1] Moreover, only one Muslim body has obtained legal personality, which is necessary to proceed in the conclusion of an agreement,[2] under the conditions of Act n. 1159/1929.

Some attempts have been made in recent years to regulate relations between the state and Islamic communities, but the political approach has not been coherent and there have been many different solutions following changes of government. For example, in 2005, a Consultative Council of Italian Islam (*Con-*

1 It is interesting to note that three different Muslim groups have presented a draft agreement to the state, and no one of them has succeeded in proceeding with negotiation: see 'Bozza d'intesa tra la Repubblica Italiana e l'Associazione Musulmani Italiani', *Quaderni di diritto e politica ecclesiastica*, 1996, no. 2, pp. 536–545; 'Bozza d'intesa tra la Repubblica Italiana e la Comunità Religiosa Islamica', *Quaderni di diritto e politica ecclesiastica*, 1998, no. 2, pp. 567–575 (also available at http://www.coreis.it/testo_dell'intesa.htm); 'Bozza di intesa fra la Repubblica italiana e l'Unione delle comunità ed organizzazioni islamiche in Italia (U.C.O.I.I.)', *Quaderni di diritto e politica ecclesiastica*, 1993, n. 2, 531–535. For a general overview of the different Muslim representatives and their attempts to conclude an *intesa* see Cilardo, Agostino, *Il diritto islamico e il sistema giuridico italiano. Le bozze di intesa tra la Repubblica italiana e le associazioni islamiche italiane*, ESI, Napoli, 2002; Mancuso, Anna Sveva, "La presenza islamica in Italia: forme di organizzazione, profili problematici e rapporti con le istituzioni", in *Stato, Chiese e pluralismo confessionale*, online journal (www.statoechiese.it), 22 February 2010. See also the bibliography in the general introduction to this volume and, among the articles in English, Silvestri, Sara, "Institutionalizing British and Italian Islam: Attitudes and Policies", in Yilmaz, Hakan—Aykaç, Çagla E. (eds.), *Perceptions of Islam in Europe*, Tauris Academic Studies, London 2012, 159–194.

2 See above, sect. 1.2.

sulta per l'Islam italiano) was established at the Ministry of Interior;[3] in 2007 and 2008 documents were prepared with the aim of reaffirming the values of a secular state and religious freedom and encouraging the foundation of a federation of Islamic groups to facilitate reaching an *intesa*. Among these documents the Ministry of the Interior promoted a Charter of Values of Citizenship and Integration in 2007; a year later, a Declaration of Intent was signed by different Muslim communities.[4] The Charter of Values of 2007 sets out a list of principles and rights recognised by the Italian constitution and legislation, e.g. freedom of religion, human dignity, equality, secularism, pluralism, respect for religious diversity. The Charter was annexed to a decree of the Ministry of the Interior, which affirms that those principles will guide government policies. The document was open for signature by the religious groups in the hope that the subscribing Islamic organisations (especially the moderate ones) would be encouraged to collaborate, merging into some sort of confederation. This prospect was (and continues to be) illusory. However, it is worth noting that the Charter has been used to establish the characteristics of integration in Italy and to identify the Muslim representatives who can participate in dialogue initiatives and in the activities of the state committees. For example, the Committee for Italian Islam, created in 2010, included only groups which had signed the Charter. This 2010 consultative committee (called the *Comitato per l'Islam Italiano*) was established at the Ministry of the Interior. Made up of 19 members (representatives of Islamic organisations, scholars, professors and journalists who are experts in Islam), it has been performing consultative functions and the Ministry has been listening to its views on some of the current topics.

After the change of government in November 2011, other initiatives by different ministers tried to develop a dialogue with Islam,[5] but without relevant

3 Ministerial decree of 10 September 2005: "Istituzione presso il Ministero dell'Interno della Consulta per l'Islam italiano" (available at http://www.olir.it/documenti/?documento=3372, last accessed 5 February 2015). The Consulta is no longer active.

4 The Declaration of Intent is merely declarative of a common interest of Muslims in developing cooperation with public authorities in the light of shared values. The document was signed on 13 March 2008; it is available at http://www.olir.it/documenti/?documento=4658 (last accessed 5 February 2015).

5 For example, the Ministry for Cooperation and Integration created, in March 2012, a permanent conference on "Religions, Culture and Integration", with Muslim organizations and experts in Islam among the participants, but open to all religions. Recently (February 2015) the Minister of the Interior gathered together several Muslim organisations for a consultative reunion (see http://www.interno.gov.it/it/notizie/alfano-incontra-i-rappresentanti-comunita-e-associazioni-islamiche-italia, last accessed 10 April 2015).

changes with regard to the relationship between the state and the Muslim community.

Decreto Ministero dell'Interno 23 Aprile 2007. *Carta dei valori della cittadinanza e dell'integrazione.*[6]
(G.U. 15 giugno 2007, n. 137)

IL MINISTRO DELL'INTERNO

[...]
Acquisita la proposta di Carta dei valori della cittadinanza e dell'integrazione elaborata dal Comitato scientifico istituito con il citato decreto 13 ottobre 2006 e la Relazione illustrativa che la accompagna;
Constatato che la Carta dei valori della cittadinanza e dell'integrazione enuclea, anche in un'ottica programmatica ed in vista di una sempre più ampia realizzazione, i principi ispiratori dell'ordinamento e della società italiana nell'accoglienza e regolazione del fenomeno migratorio in un quadro di pluralismo culturale e religioso;
Ritenuto che la Carta possa costituire, anche alla luce di analoghe esperienze ed iniziative avviate in altri Paesi europei, un utile strumento di orientamento dell'azione dell'Amministrazione dell'interno per l'integrazione dei soggetti dell'immigrazione nella società italiana e per favorire la coesione sociale attraverso le più idonee garanzie civili e sociali, in coerenza con il quadro normativo costituzionale, comunitario, e internazionale sui diritti umani;
[...]

Decreta:

Art. 1.
1. Il Ministero dell'interno, nell'esercizio delle proprie attribuzioni, si ispira alla Carta dei valori della cittadinanza e dell'integrazione, di seguito denominata Carta dei valori, il cui testo è riportato nell'allegato che forma parte integrante del presente decreto.
2. Il Ministero dell'interno orienta le relazioni con le comunità degli immigrati e religiose al comune rispetto dei principi della Carta dei valori, nella prospettiva dell'integrazione e della coesione sociale.

6 http://www.olir.it/documenti/?documento=4659 (last accessed 1 February 2015).

Art. 2.
1. È istituito il Consiglio scientifico incaricato di approfondire e proporre le più opportune iniziative per la conoscenza, la diffusione della Carta dei valori ed i successivi interventi e di studiare le soluzioni più adeguate per l'armonica convivenza delle comunità dell'immigrazione e religiose nella società italiana.
2. Nell'espletamento del suo mandato il Consiglio scientifico procede anche mediante incontri consultivi con esponenti delle associazioni ed organizzazioni operanti nel mondo delle comunità immigrate, con esponenti delle diverse confessioni ed organizzazioni religiose, con i componenti della Consulta per l'Islam italiano, che, aderendo alla Carta dei valori, intendano partecipare, nella propria autonomia, alla diffusione e attuazione della Carta.
3. Con separato provvedimento si procederà alla costituzione e alla disciplina del Consiglio.

Allegato
CARTA DEI VALORI DELLA CITTADINANZA E DELL'INTEGRAZIONE

L'Italia, comunità di persone e di valori.
L'Italia è uno dei Paesi più antichi d'Europa che affonda le radici nella cultura classica della Grecia e di Roma. Essa si è evoluta nell'orizzonte del cristianesimo che ha permeato la sua storia e, insieme con l'ebraismo, ha preparato l'apertura verso la modernità e i principi di libertà e di giustizia.
I valori su cui si fonda la società italiana sono frutto dell'impegno di generazioni di uomini e di donne di diversi orientamenti, laici e religiosi, e sono scritti nella Costituzione democratica del 1947. La Costituzione rappresenta lo spartiacque nei confronti del totalitarismo, e dell'antisemitismo che ha avvelenato l'Europa del XX secolo e perseguitato il popolo ebraico e la sua cultura.
La Costituzione è fondata sul rispetto della dignità umana ed è ispirata ai principi di libertà ed eguaglianza validi per chiunque si trovi a vivere sul territorio italiano. Partendo dalla Costituzione l'Italia ha partecipato alla costruzione dell'Europa unita e delle sue istituzioni. I Trattati e le Convenzioni europee contribuiscono a realizzare un ordine internazionale basato sui diritti umani e sulla eguaglianza e solidarietà tra i popoli.
La posizione geografica dell'Italia, la tradizione ebraico-cristiana, le istituzioni libere e democratiche che la governano, sono alla base del suo atteggiamento di accoglienza verso altre popolazioni. Immersa nel Mediterraneo, l'Italia è stata sempre crocevia di popoli e culture diverse, e la sua popolazione presenta ancora oggi i segni di questa diversità.

Tutto ciò che costituisce il patrimonio dell'Italia, le sue bellezze artistiche e naturali, le risorse economiche e culturali, le sue istituzioni democratiche sono al servizio degli uomini, delle donne, dei giovani, e delle future generazioni. La nostra Carta costituzionale tutela e promuove i diritti umani inalienabili, per sostenere i più deboli, per garantire lo sviluppo delle capacità e attitudini di lavoro, morali, spirituali, di ogni persona.

Dignità della persona, diritti e doveri.

1. L'Italia è impegnata perché ogni persona sin dal primo momento in cui si trova sul territorio italiano possa fruire dei diritti fondamentali, senza distinzione di sesso, etnia, religione, condizioni sociali. Al tempo stesso, ogni persona che vive in Italia deve rispettare i valori su cui poggia la società, i diritti degli altri, i doveri di solidarietà richiesti dalle leggi. Alle condizioni previste dalla legge, l'Italia offre asilo e protezione a quanti, nei propri paesi, sono perseguitati o impediti nell'esercizio delle libertà fondamentali.
2. Nel prevedere parità di diritti e di doveri per tutti, la legge offre il suo sostegno a chi subisce discriminazioni, o vive in stato di bisogno, in particolare alle donne e ai minori, rimovendo gli ostacoli che impediscono il pieno sviluppo della persona.
3. I diritti di libertà, e i diritti sociali, che il nostro ordinamento ha maturato nel tempo devono estendersi a tutti gli immigrati. E' garantito il diritto alla vita dal suo inizio fino al compimento naturale, e il diritto alla salute con le cure gratuite quando siano necessarie; una protezione speciale è assicurata alla maternità e all'infanzia. Il diritto all'istruzione è riconosciuto quale strumento indispensabile per la crescita personale e l'inserimento nella società.
4. L'uomo e la donna hanno pari dignità e fruiscono degli stessi diritti dentro e fuori la famiglia. Alle donne, agli uomini, ai giovani immigrati l'Italia offre un cammino di integrazione rispettoso delle identità di ciascuno, e che porti coloro che scelgono di stabilirsi nel nostro Paese a partecipare attivamente alla vita sociale.
5. L'immigrato può, alle condizioni previste dalla legge, diventare cittadino italiano. Per ottenere la cittadinanza nei tempi previsti dalla legge occorre conoscere la lingua italiana e gli elementi essenziali della storia e della cultura nazionali, e condividere i principi che regolano la nostra società. Vivere sulla stessa terra vuol dire poter essere pienamente cittadini insieme e far propri con lealtà e coerenza valori e responsabilità comuni.

Diritti sociali. Lavoro e salute.

[...]

Diritti sociali. Scuola, istruzione, informazione.

11. I bambini e i ragazzi hanno il diritto e il dovere di frequentare la scuola dell'obbligo, per inserirsi a parità di diritti nella società e divenirne soggetti attivi. E' dovere di ogni genitore, italiano o straniero, sostenere i figli negli studi, in primo luogo iscrivendoli alla scuola dell'obbligo, che inizia con la scuola primaria fino ai 16 anni.

12. L'insegnamento è diretto alla formazione della persona e promuove la conoscenza dei diritti fondamentali e l'educazione alla legalità, le relazioni amichevoli tra gli uomini, il rispetto e la benevolenza verso ogni forma di vita esistente. Anche per favorire la condivisione degli stessi valori, la scuola prevede programmi per la conoscenza della storia, della cultura, e dei principi delle tradizioni italiana ed europea. Per un insegnamento adeguato al pluralismo della società è altresì essenziale, in una prospettiva interculturale, promuovere la conoscenza della cultura e della religione di appartenenza dei ragazzi e delle loro famiglie.

13. La scuola promuove la conoscenza e l'integrazione tra tutti i ragazzi, il superamento dei pregiudizi, e la crescita comune dei giovani evitando divisioni e discriminazioni. L'insegnamento è impartito nel rispetto delle opinioni religiose o ideali dei ragazzi e delle famiglie e, a determinate condizioni, prevede corsi di insegnamento religioso scelti volontariamente dagli alunni o dai loro genitori.

14. Sulla base degli stessi valori, spetta anche ai mezzi d'informazione favorire la conoscenza dell'immigrazione, delle sue componenti culturali e religiose, contrastando pregiudizi e xenofobie. Il loro ruolo è essenziale per diffondere un pluralismo culturale rispettoso delle tradizioni e dei valori basilari della società italiana.

15. E' garantito il diritto di enti e privati di istituire scuole o corsi scolastici, purché non discriminino gli alunni per motivi etnici o confessionali, e assicurino un insegnamento in armonia con i principi generali dell'istruzione, e i diritti umani che spettano alle persone. Ogni tipo di insegnamento, comunque impartito a livello pubblico o privato, deve rispettare le convinzioni di ciascuno e tendere a unire gli uomini anziché a dividerli.

Famiglia, nuove generazioni.

16. L'Italia riconosce i diritti della famiglia come società naturale fondata sul matrimonio, e considera l'educazione familiare strumento necessario per la crescita delle nuove generazioni.

17. Il matrimonio è fondato sulla eguaglianza di diritti e di responsabilità tra marito e moglie, ed è per questo a struttura monogamica. La monogamia unisce due vite e le rende corresponsabili di ciò che realizzano insieme, a

cominciare dalla crescita dei figli. L'Italia proibisce la poligamia come contraria ai diritti della donna, in accordo anche con i principi affermati dalle istituzioni europee.
18. L'ordinamento italiano proibisce ogni forma di coercizione e di violenza dentro e fuori la famiglia, e tutela la dignità della donna in tutte le sue manifestazioni e in ogni momento della vita associativa. Base dell'unione coniugale è la libertà matrimoniale che spetta ai giovani, e comporta il divieto di coercizioni e di matrimoni forzati, o tra bambini.
19. L'Italia tutela la libertà dei minori nello sviluppo della propria personalità, che si realizza anche nell'incontro con altri giovani e nella partecipazione alle attività sociali. Il principio di eguaglianza non è conciliabile con le pretese di separare, a motivo dell'appartenenza confessionale, uomini e donne, ragazzi e ragazze, nei servizi pubblici e nell'espletamento delle attività lavorative.

Laicità e libertà religiosa.
20. L'Italia è un Paese laico fondato sul riconoscimento della piena libertà religiosa individuale e collettiva. La libertà religiosa riconosciuta ad ogni persona, cittadino o straniero, e alle comunità religiose. La religione e la convinzione non possono essere motivo di discriminazione nella vita sociale.
21. Tutte le confessioni religiose sono egualmente libere davanti alla legge. Lo Stato laico riconosce il contributo positivo che le religioni recano alla collettività e intende valorizzare il patrimonio morale e spirituale di ciascuna di esse. L'Italia favorisce il dialogo interreligioso e interculturale per far crescere il rispetto della dignità umana, e contribuire al superamento di pregiudizi e intolleranza. La Costituzione prevede accordi tra Stato e confessioni religiose per regolare le loro specifiche condizioni giuridiche.
22. I principi di libertà e i diritti della persona non possono essere violati nel nome di alcuna religione. È esclusa ogni forma di violenza, o istigazione alla violenza, comunque motivata dalla religione. La legge, civile e penale, è eguale per tutti, a prescindere dalla religione di ciascuno, ed unica è la giurisdizione dei tribunali per chi si trovi sul territorio italiano.
23. La libertà religiosa e di coscienza comprende il diritto di avere una fede religiosa, o di non averla, di essere praticante o non praticante, di cambiare religione, di diffonderla convincendo gli altri, di unirsi in organizzazioni confessionali. È pienamente garantita la libertà di culto, e ciascuno può adempiere alle prescrizioni religiose purché non contrastino con le norme penali e con i diritti degli altri.
24. L'ordinamento tutela la libertà di ricerca, di critica e di discussione, anche in materia religiosa, e proibisce l'offesa verso la religione e il sentimento

religioso delle persone. Per la legge dello Stato, la differenza di religione e di convinzione non è di ostacolo alla celebrazione del matrimonio.
25. Movendo dalla propria tradizione religiosa e culturale, l'Italia rispetta i simboli, e i segni, di tutte le religioni.
Nessuno può ritenersi offeso dai segni e dai simboli di religioni diverse dalla sua. Come stabilito dalle Carte internazionali, è giusto educare i giovani a rispettare le convinzioni religiose degli altri, senza vedere in esse fattori di divisione degli esseri umani.
26. In Italia non si pongono restrizioni all'abbigliamento della persona, purché liberamente scelto, e non lesivo della sua dignità.
Non sono accettabili forme di vestiario che coprono il volto perché ciò impedisce il riconoscimento della persona e la ostacola nell'entrare in rapporto con gli altri.

L'impegno internazionale dell'Italia.
27. In coerenza con questi principi l'Italia svolge nel mondo una politica di pace e di rispetto di tutti i popoli, per promuovere la convivenza tra le nazioni, per sconfiggere la guerra e il terrorismo.
L'Italia è impegnata in campo internazionale per tutelare le ricchezze di vita e di ambiente del pianeta
28. L'Italia ripudia la guerra come strumento di soluzione delle controversie internazionali, le armi di distruzione di massa, e ogni forma di tortura o di pene degradanti per la dignità umana. Essa condanna l'antisemitismo, che ha portato al genocidio del popolo ebraico, e ogni tendenza razzista che vuole dividere gli uomini e umiliare i più deboli. L'Italia rifiuta tutte le manifestazioni di xenofobia che si esprimono di volta in volta nella islamofobia o in pregiudizi verso popolazioni che vengono da altre parti del mondo.
[...]
Roma, 23 aprile 2007

2.2 The Legal Status of Islamic Organisations in Italy

As has already been said, there is no specific document on the legal status of Islam in Italy. One can refer to Act n. 1159 of 1929 (see sect. 1.3) about the recognition of religious bodies or to legislation on associations and non-profit-making organisations, which is the most common legal structure used by Islamic groups.

The only Islamic body registered under Act n. 1159/1929 is the Islamic Cultural Centre of Italy (*Centro Islamico culturale d'Italia*), where the Mosque of Rome is located (thus the Centre is also known as the "Mosque of Rome"). The recognition is provided by a decree of the President of the Republic (d.P.R.). The d.P.R. states that the Islamic Centre has legal personality in Italy and that its statute has been approved and registered as a public act through a notary. Article 3 recalls that, according to the legislation of 1929–1930, legal representatives of the Centre shall be domiciled in Italy.

Decreto Presidente Repubblica 21 dicembre 1974, n. 712. ***Riconoscimento della personalità giuridica dell'ente "Centro Islamico culturale d'Italia" con sede in Roma Via A. Casella n. 51***[7]

Art. 1
È riconosciuta la personalità giuridica dell'ente "Centro Islamico culturale d'Italia" con sede in Roma Via A. Casella n. 51.

Art. 2
È approvato lo statuto aggiornato dell'ente, composto di venti articoli redatto per atto pubblico del 4 agosto 1972 n. 32590, a rogito notaio Marco Panvini Rosati, registrato a Roma il 7 agosto 1972 al n. 8728 vol. 1621, atti pubblici che sarà munito di visto e sottoscritto dal Ministro proponente.

Art. 3
In conformità dell'art. 10 3° comma del regio decreto 28 febbraio 1930 n. 289 i legittimi rappresentanti dell'ente di cui all'articolo 17 dello statuto aggiornato devono avere il domicilio in Italia.
Gli argomenti previsti dall'articolo 19 del predetto Statuto devono essere deliberati dall'assemblea straordinari dei soci con la maggioranza stabilita dall'articolo 3° comma del codice civile.
[...]

7 http://www.olir.it/documenti/?documento=5242 (last accessed 1 February 2015).

CHAPTER 3

State Support for Islamic Religious Communities

In 1984 the revision of the 1929 Concordat between Italy and the Holy See marked the beginning of a new system of state financial support for religious communities. Act n. 121 of 1985 ratifying the "new Concordat" of 1984 and Act n. 222 of 1985, ratifying an agreement on Church entities and properties, introduced the system of *otto per mille* ("eight thousandths") and the possibility for taxpayers to deduct from their taxable income donations to the central ecclesiastical body for the remuneration of the clergy. As long as non-Catholic religious communities have signed an agreement with the state, they can also access these two mechanisms of state funding (with few differences among different *intese*); as a result, the system of *otto per mille* distributes the 0.8 per cent of the state revenue from income tax among the religions that have concluded an agreement, in proportion to choices made by taxpayers; moreover, donations to various religious institutions are deductible.

Access to both systems of state funding (*otto per mille* and donations) is subject to the conclusion of an agreement with the state: this excludes from these forms of financial support Islamic organisations which have not signed an *intesa*.

Italian legislation on taxation gives the religious denominations and their bodies numerous privileges.[1] Organisations with religious purposes are treated in the same way as organisations with social purposes: this main principle is sanctioned by the agreement of 1984 between the state and the Catholic Church and by the legislation of 1929–1930 on non-Catholic denominations. In particular, Article 12 of Royal Decree n. 289 of 1930 states that the bodies of "admitted cults" which have religious aims shall enjoy the same fiscal regime as organisations with welfare and educational aims.

Provisions on taxes and on fiscal exemptions are fragmentary and subject to frequent changes and amendments; therefore only some examples will be provided here. Among the fiscal exemptions for religious bodies we can mention a rebate of 50 per cent of corporation tax (Art. 6 of d.P.R. n. 601 of 1973[2]); exemption from value added tax (*imposta sul valore aggiunto*, IVA-VAT[3]); exemption

1 For an overview and some examples of tax exemptions see Ferrari, Alessandro, and Ferrari, Silvio, "Religion and the Secular State, The Italian Case", pp. 462 ff.

2 Decree of the President of the Republic n. 601/1973; see the document reproduced here below.

3 Decree of the President of the Republic n. 633/1972, art. 10.1, n. 12 (see below).

from some local taxation, such as the property tax (ICI-IMU, *imposta comunale sull'incremento di valore dei beni immobili*).[4] The last has created concerns and a quite vast debate on the application of the tax to the buildings of religious denominations that are used for both commercial purposes and religious activities.[5]

Exemptions are granted also to other types of associations and organisations with social purposes. This is relevant for Islam because, as has already been said, Muslim organisations often operate in Italy as ONLUS (organisations without economic purposes, established by Legislative Decree n. 460 of 1997) or simple associations.[6] Legislation in force provides for a special legal regime, as well as for fiscal exemptions in favour of associations, organisations and agencies with welfare and non-profit-making aims (e.g. Art. 12 of the decree on ONLUS establishes an allowance on income tax).

Recently, a system of indirect state financial support has been introduced for non-profit-making organisations: the *cinque per mille*. According to the financial law (*legge finanziaria*) passed in December 2005, taxpayers can allocate a portion of 0.5 per cent of their income tax to certain categories of organisations with social purposes: among them are non-profit-making bodies linked to religious communities, in so far as they fulfil the requirements of the legislation, signing up to a register at the Tax Agency.

Regio Decreto 28 febbraio 1930, n. 289. ***Norme per l'attuazione della legge 24 giugno 1929, n. 1159/1929, sui culti ammessi nello Stato e per il coordinamento di essa con le altre leggi dello Stato***

Art. 12
Relativamente agli atti compiuti nell'interesse di istituti, eretti in ente morale, dai culti ammessi nello Stato, il fine di culto è, a tutti gli effetti tributari, equiparato a quello di beneficenza e di istruzione

Decreto del Presidente della Repubblica 26 ottobre 1972, n. 633. ***Istituzione e disciplina dell'imposta sul valore aggiunto***
(GU n. 292 del 11-11-1972—Suppl. Ordinario)[7]

4 See legislative decrees n. 504 of 1992 and n. 23 of 2011 and Act 22 December 2011 n. 214.

5 Cf. Ventura, Marco, *Religion and Law in Italy*, Alphen aan den Rijn: Wolters Kluwer, 2013, pp. 190 ff.

6 See sect. 1.4.

7 www.normattiva.it/uri-res/N2Ls?urn:nir:stato:decreto.del.presidente.della.repubblica:1972-10-26;633!vig=2015-02-06 (last accessed 6 February 2015).

Art. 10. *Operazioni esenti dall'imposta*
Sono esenti dall'imposta:
[...]
12) le cessioni di cui al n. 4) dell'art. 2 fatte ad enti pubblici, associazioni riconosciute o fondazioni aventi esclusivamente finalità di assistenza, beneficenza, educazione, istruzione, studio o ricerca scientifica e alle ONLUS;
[...]

Decreto del Presidente della Repubblica 29 settembre 1973, n. 601. *Disciplina delle agevolazioni tributarie*

Art. 6. *Riduzione dell'imposta sul reddito delle persone giuridiche*[8]
1. L'imposta sul reddito delle persone giuridiche è ridotta alla metà nei confronti dei seguenti soggetti:
a) enti e istituti di assistenza sociale, società di mutuo soccorso, enti ospedalieri, enti di assistenza e beneficenza;
b) istituti di istruzione e istituti di studio e sperimentazione di interesse generale che non hanno fine di lucro, corpi scientifici, accademie, fondazioni e associazioni storiche, letterarie, scientifiche, di esperienze e ricerche aventi scopi esclusivamente culturali;
c) enti il cui fine è equiparato per legge ai fini di beneficenza o di istruzione.
2. Per i soggetti di cui al comma 1 la riduzione compete a condizione che abbiano personalità giuridica.

Decreto legislativo 4 dicembre 1997, n. 460. *Riordino della disciplina tributaria degli enti non commerciali e delle organizzazioni non lucrative di utilità sociale* (*ONLUS*)[9]

Art. 12. *Agevolazioni ai fini delle imposte sui redditi*
1. Nel testo unico delle imposte sui redditi, approvato con decreto del Presidente della Repubblica 22 dicembre 1986, n. 917, dopo l'articolo 111-bis, introdotto dall'articolo 6, comma 1, del presente decreto, è inserito il seguente:
"Art. 111-ter (Organizzazioni non lucrative di utilità sociale).
1. Per le organizzazioni non lucrative di utilità sociale (ONLUS), ad eccezione delle società cooperative, non costituisce esercizio di attività commerciale lo

---

8 Text as amended by Art. 66.8 of the decree-law n. 331 of 1993, converted into Act n. 427 of 29 October 1993 (in G.U. 29/10/1993, n. 255).

9 www.normattiva.it/uri-res/N2Ls?urn:nir:stato:decreto.legislativo:1997-12-04;460 (last accessed 26 January 2015).

svolgimento delle attività istituzionali nel perseguimento di esclusive finalità di solidarietà sociale.
2. I proventi derivanti dall'esercizio delle attività direttamente connesse non concorrono alla formazione del reddito imponibile.".

Legge 23 dicembre 2005, n. 266. ***Disposizioni per la formazione del bilancio annuale e pluriennale dello Stato (legge finanziaria 2006)***
(GU n. 302 del 29-12-2005—Suppl. Ordinario n. 211)

Art. 1, n. 337[10]
Per l'anno finanziario 2006, ed a titolo iniziale e sperimentale, fermo quanto già dovuto dai contribuenti a titolo di imposta sul reddito delle persone fisiche, una quota pari al 5 per mille dell'imposta stessa è destinata in base alla scelta del contribuente alle seguenti finalità:
a) sostegno del volontariato e delle altre organizzazioni non lucrative di utilità sociale di cui all'articolo 10 del decreto legislativo 4 dicembre 1997, n. 460, e successive modificazioni, nonché delle associazioni di promozione sociale iscritte nei registri nazionale, regionali e provinciali previsti dall'articolo 7, commi 1, 2, 3 e 4, della legge 7 dicembre 2000, n. 383, e delle associazioni e fondazioni riconosciute che operano nei settori di cui all'articolo 10, comma 1, lettera a), del decreto legislativo 4 dicembre 1997, n. 460;
b) finanziamento della ricerca scientifica e dell'università;
c) finanziamento della ricerca sanitaria;
d) attività sociali svolte dal comune di residenza del contribuente.

10 This article establishes the system of "*cinque per mille*". Art. 1, n. 340 stipulates that a Decree will establish the conditions for accessing the "register" of organisations that will benefit from this system of state support. The decree regulating these specific conditions is the Decree of the President of the Council of Ministers (DPCM) of 20 of January 2006: *Definizione della modalità di destinazione della quota pari al cinque per mille dell'imposta sul reddito delle persone fisiche, in base alla scelta del contribuente, per finalità di volontariato, ricerca scientifica e dell'università, ricerca sanitaria e attività sociali svolte dal comune di residenza.*

CHAPTER 4

Muslims in Integration Law

Many Muslims in Italy are immigrants without Italian citizenship; thus, in public opinion and in public debate there is confusion between their being Muslims and being immigrants. Islam is often seen as a religion that differs from the traditions of the majority of Italians; on the other hand, integration issues are often considered in the sole light of immigration policies and in the actions about the presence of foreign people in Italy, without taking account of religious aspects.[1] The social role and inclusion of different religions (and Islam among them) is hardly ever a separate and specific question in policies and legislation on integration.

Sometimes we can find a general recommendation about respecting religious pluralism and the non-discrimination principle (for example in the guidelines for integration at school, published by the Ministry of University and Public Education[2]). In documents on immigration and the integration of immigrants, provisions that are relevant also for religious rights are included, for example the prohibition of racial and religious discrimination (e.g. Articles 43 and 44 of the legislative decree n. 268/1998 which is the unified text on immigration[3]).

The Charter of Values (see *supra*, ch. 2) has tried to pave the way for the building of an Italian Islam, highlighting the common values of the country and asking Muslim communities to adhere to those values. However, this has not given effect to practical consequences or new policies.

At the local level, some Regions have included in their statutes (or in specific regional acts) principles guiding the policies on the integration of immigrants and foreign residents, mentioning for example the prohibition of religious discrimination.[4] Sometimes, Regions or other local institutions provide for

1 See above, the general introduction and the related bibliography.

2 http://www.olir.it/documenti/?documento=6308 (last accessed 27 January 2015).

3 See ch. 10.

4 For example: Regione Campania, statute of 2009 (here below) and regional Act n. 6 of 8 February 2010 (here below); Regione Lombardia, statute of 2008 (available at http://www.olir.it/documenti/?documento=4685, last accessed 27 January 2015); Regione Marche, regional act n. 13 of 26 May 2009 *"Disposizioni a sostegno dei diritti e dell'integrazione dei cittadini stranieri immigrati"* art. 1 (available at http://www.olir.it/documenti/?documento=5024, last accessed 27 January 2015); Regione Toscana, regional act n. 29 of 2009, art. 69 (see below).

more concrete policies and actions about integration, making reference also to religious aspects (for example: the presence of different religions at school,[5] with education programmes, dietary provision in the canteens and holidays;[6] the promotion of cultural diversity through cultural activities and projects;[7] assistance to foreign residents, also from a religious point of view[8]).

In some Regions, there are specific bodies aimed at promoting integration and fighting against discrimination, in which the participation of religious communities is anticipated,[9] or consultative bodies created especially for dialogue among religions (among them Islam).[10]

Regione Calabria, legge regionale 19 ottobre 2004, n. 25. ***Statuto della Regione Calabria***

(Bollettino Ufficiale della Regione—Supplemento straordinario n. 6 del 23.10.2004)[11]

Art. 2. *Principi e finalità*

[...]

2. La Regione ispira in particolare la sua azione al raggiungimento dei seguenti obiettivi:

5 Regione Toscana, regional act n. 2 of 23 January 2013: "Modifiche alla legge regionale 26 luglio 2002, n. 32 (Testo unico della normativa della Regione Toscana in materia di educazione, istruzione, orientamento, formazione professionale e lavoro), in materia di sistema regionale dei servizi educativi per la prima infanzia e di tirocini" (http://www.olir.it/documenti/?documento=6096, last accessed 27 January 2015).

6 Regione Toscana, regional act n. 29 of 2009, Art. 53 (see below).

7 Regione Lazio, regional act n. 10 of 14 July 2008 "Disposizioni per la promozione e la tutela dell'esercizio dei diritti civili e sociali e per la piena uguaglianza dei cittadini stranieri immigrati", provides for actions on integration and intercultural mediation, at school (available at http://www.olir.it/documenti/?documento=4759, last accessed 27 January 2015); the statute of Region Calabria, published below, mentions cooperation with religious denominations and the valorization of ethnic and religious minorities.

8 Again Act of Regione Toscana n. 29/2009, Art. 53 (reproduced below).

9 Provincia Autonoma di Bolzano—Alto Adige, decree of the President of the Province n. 36 of 15 October 2012 ("Regolamento di esecuzione concernente il Centro di tutela contro le discriminazioni", at http://www.olir.it/ricerca/getdocumentopdf.php?lang=ita&Form_object_id=6017, last accessed 2 February 2015).

10 For example the Consultative body of the City of Florence for interreligious dialogue: see the deliberation of the City Council published here below.

11 Available at http://www.regione.calabria.it/allegati/documenti/statuto_regcal.pdf (last accessed 28 January 2015).

[...]
p) la tutela e la valorizzazione delle minoranze etniche, linguistiche e religiose presenti in Calabria, con particolare riguardo alle popolazioni di origine albanese, grecanica, occitanica e rom;

Art. 4. *Partecipazione popolare*
1. La Regione promuove la partecipazione dei singoli, delle formazioni sociali e politiche e di tutte le componenti della Comunità calabrese, nonché delle comunità dei calabresi nel mondo alla vita delle istituzioni regionali, al fine di realizzare una democrazia compiuta e lo sviluppo civile delle popolazioni.
2. A tal fine, la legge stabilisce procedure e criteri idonei per rendere effettiva la partecipazione, assicurando servizi e strutture regionali e prevedendo la consultazione di organismi rappresentativi di istanze sociali diffuse.
3. Negli ambiti di propria competenza, la Regione può attivare particolari forme di cooperazione con le confessioni religiose presenti in Calabria.

Regione Campania. Legge regionale n. 6, 28 maggio 2009: *Statuto della Regione Campania*[12]

Art. 1. *Principi fondamentali*
[...]
2. La Regione Campania ispira la propria azione ai principi della democrazia, dello stato di diritto e della centralità della persona umana. Garantisce e promuove i principi di uguaglianza, solidarietà, libertà, giustizia sociale e pari opportunità tra donne e uomini. Partecipa alla promozione della pace con iniziative legislative di informazione ed educazione in conformità al principio costituzionale del ripudio della guerra quale mezzo di risoluzione delle controversie internazionali. La Regione contribuisce al mantenimento di tali valori nel rispetto e con il contributo delle diversità e delle minoranze.
3. La Regione Campania garantisce la partecipazione democratica di tutti i cittadini e le cittadine, degli enti, delle associazioni, delle formazioni sociali e delle istituzioni territoriali alla determinazione ed attuazione dell'indirizzo politico regionale.
[...]

12 Available at http://www.consiglio.regione.campania.it/cms/CM_PORTALE_CRC/servlet/Docs?dir=statuto&file=statuto.pdf (last accessed 28 January 2015).

5. La Regione, crogiolo delle antiche civiltà italica, etrusca, greca, romana e sannita, svolge la funzione di grande mediatrice fra oriente ed occidente conferitale dal carattere universale della sua cultura.

Art. 4. *Principio di uguaglianza*
1. La Regione riconosce e garantisce i diritti di libertà e di uguaglianza previsti dalla Costituzione e dalle convenzioni internazionali riconosciute nel nostro ordinamento ponendoli a fondamento e limite di tutte le proprie attività.
2. La Regione concorre a rimuovere gli ostacoli di ordine economico, sociale, culturale, sessuale, etnico e religioso che limitano l'uguaglianza e la libertà dei cittadini.
3. La Regione riconosce l'apporto derivante dalle diverse storie, dalle diverse culture e dalle radici religiose cristiane delle comunità campane e considera l'incontro tra le differenti civiltà, religioni e culture del Mediterraneo quale fondamentale strumento di formazione e crescita di una comunità pluralista ed interetnica.

Art. 8. *Obiettivi*
1. La Regione promuove ogni utile iniziativa per favorire:
[...]
m) la tutela e la valorizzazione del patrimonio culturale della Regione, delle diversità culturali, religiose e linguistiche, nonché di quelle relative ai dialetti locali;
[...]
o) la realizzazione di un elevato livello delle prestazioni concernenti i diritti sociali nonché il godimento dei diritti politici e sociali degli immigrati, degli stranieri profughi rifugiati e degli apolidi, ivi compreso il diritto di voto, per quanto compatibile con la Costituzione;
[...]

Regione Campania, Legge regionale 8 febbraio 2010 n. 6. ***Norme per l'inclusione sociale, economica e culturale delle persone straniere presenti in Campania.***
(in B.U. Campania 19 febbraio 2010, n. 16)[13]

Art. 1. *Principi generali e finalità*
1. La regione Campania nell'ambito delle proprie competenze e in conformità con le disposizioni legislative nazionali ed europee:

13 http://www.olir.it/documenti/?documento=5449 (last accessed 1 February 2015).

a) collabora con le competenti autorità centrali e periferiche dello Stato al fine di assicurare un efficace coordinamento degli interventi in materia di immigrazione;
b) concorre ad assicurare ai cittadini di Stati non appartenenti all'Unione europea e agli apolidi, che dimorano nel territorio della regione, l'effettivo godimento dei diritti fondamentali della persona umana previsti dalle norme statali, comunitarie e internazionali;
c) promuove iniziative rivolte a garantire alle persone straniere regolarmente soggiornanti in Campania condizioni di uguaglianza nel godimento dei diritti civili e sociali con i cittadini italiani ed a rimuovere le cause che ne ostacolano l'inserimento nel tessuto sociale, culturale ed economico;
d) concorre a prevenire e a rimuovere ogni forma di razzismo e di xenofobìa.
2. La Regione, le province e i comuni garantiscono alle persone straniere presenti sul territorio campano la pari opportunità di accesso ai servizi, il riconoscimento e la valorizzazione della parità di genere ed il principio di indirizzare l'azione amministrativa all'effettivo esercizio dei diritti. A tal fine, le politiche della Regione e degli enti locali sono finalizzate:
a) alla rimozione degli ostacoli per l'effettivo inserimento sociale, culturale e politico;
b) al riconoscimento delle identità culturali, religiose e linguistiche, ispirandosi ai principi di uguaglianza e libertà religiosa secondo gli articoli 8, 19 e 20 della Costituzione;
c) alla valorizzazione della consapevolezza dei diritti e dei doveri, come disciplinata dalle convenzioni internazionali in materia dei diritti dell'uomo, dall'ordinamento europeo ed italiano.
3. La Regione organizza un sistema di tutela e promozione sociale delle persone straniere attraverso iniziative volte a:
a) accrescere l'informazione e la sensibilizzazione sul fenomeno migratorio promuovendo, altresì, la conoscenza delle culture di provenienza e la loro valorizzazione;
b) assicurare pari opportunità di accesso all'abitazione, al lavoro, all'istruzione ed alla formazione professionale, alla conoscenza delle opportunità connesse all'avvio di attività autonome e imprenditoriali, alle prestazioni sanitarie ed assistenziali nonché alle attività di mediazione interculturale;
[...]

Art. 13. *Misure contro la discriminazione*
1. La Regione promuove e sostiene azioni di monitoraggio, assistenza e tutela legale per le vittime di ogni forma di discriminazione diretta ed indiretta, fondata sulla xenofobia, la razza, l'origine etnica o l'appartenenza religiosa non-

ché per le vittime delle situazioni di violenza o di grave sfruttamento, anche in ambito lavorativo, di cui all'articolo 18 del decreto legislativo n. 286/1998 e della legge 11 agosto 2003 n. 228 (Misure contro la tratta di persone).
[...]

Regione Toscana. Legge regionale 09 giugno 2009, n. 29.
Norme per l'accoglienza, l'integrazione partecipe e la tutela dei cittadini stranieri nella Regione Toscana.[14]

Art. 53.
La Regione, nell'ambito delle proprie competenze, promuove interventi volti a favorire:
a) l'assistenza religiosa nei luoghi di detenzione e di pena, nelle strutture ospedaliere e di cura a richiesta degli interessati;
b) l'assegnazione di spazi cimiteriali per la sepoltura e lo svolgimento dei riti funebri;
c) la professione del culto in luoghi adeguati;
d) l'assegnazione di spazi per la macellazione rituale nel rispetto della normativa vigente;
e) il rispetto delle norme alimentari previste dalle diverse tradizioni religiose nelle mense pubbliche;
f) lo sviluppo di relazioni tra organizzazioni sindacali e organizzazioni datoriali per l'esame di possibili intese finalizzate a consentire l'osservanza nei luoghi di lavoro delle prescrizioni rituali e delle festività previste dalle differenti tradizioni religiose.

Art. 69.
La Regione, in collaborazione con province, comuni e con le organizzazioni del terzo settore, adotta misure contro la discriminazione per motivi razziali, etnici, nazionali o religiosi, nell'ambito delle politiche di contrasto contro tutte le forme di discriminazione.

Comune di Firenze. Deliberazione del Consiglio Comunale n. 12 del 16 febbraio 2009. *Regolamento della Consulta per il Dialogo con le Confessioni Religiose del Comune di Firenze*[15]

---

14 http://www.olir.it/documenti/index.php?argomento=0&documento=5040 (last accessed 1 February 2015).

15 Available at http://www.olir.it/documenti/?documento=5443 (last accessed 28 January 2015).

Art. 1. Istituzione
1. E' istituita presso il Comune di Firenze la Consulta per il Dialogo con le Confessioni Religiose, in sostituzione della Conferenza Permanente per il dialogo tra le Confessioni Religiose.

Art. 2. Composizione e Durata
1. La Consulta per il Dialogo con le Confessioni Religiose è composta dai rappresentanti sia delle confessioni religiose presenti sul territorio del Comune di Firenze e aventi rapporti con lo Stato italiano ai sensi della vigente legislazione in materia, sia di altre confessioni che, indipendentemente dal requisito di cui sopra, possano comunque dimostrare una presenza significativa e radicata nel territorio del Comune e che hanno espresso la volontà di far parte di questo organismo, mediante la partecipazione di un proprio rappresentante, in occasione dell'elaborazione, discussione ed approvazione del presente regolamento. Oltre a questi, sono membri di diritto della Consulta: il Presidente della v Commissione Consiliare o un suo delegato, scelto tra i componenti della Commissione ed il Direttore/Responsabile del Centro di In-Formazione Religiosa; in prima istanza fanno parte della Consulta i rappresentanti delle Confessioni religiose già partecipi della Conferenza Permanente.
2. Altre confessioni religiose presenti sul territorio del Comune di Firenze e aventi rapporti con lo Stato italiano ai sensi della vigente legislazione in materia, così come altre confessioni che, indipendentemente dal requisito di cui sopra, possano comunque dimostrare una presenza significativa e radicata nel territorio del Comune, possono presentare domanda per entrare a far parte della Consulta per il Dialogo con le Confessioni Religiose, mediante la partecipazione di un proprio rappresentante ai lavori della stessa. L'accoglimento della domanda è disposto dal Presidente della v Commissione Consiliare, sentita la Consulta e previo accertamento del possesso dei requisiti richiesti.
3. I membri della Consulta per il Dialogo con le Confessioni Religiose restano in carica tre anni.

Art. 3. Struttura
1. Per favorire il regolare corso delle sue attività, la Consulta si avvale del seguente organigramma:
a) L'Assemblea dei delegati delle confessioni religiose;
b) La Commissione direttiva.

Art. 4. L'Assemblea dei delegati delle Confessioni Religiose
1. L'assemblea è composta da un rappresentante per ogni confessione religiosa, con diritto di voto.
2. I lavori dell'Assemblea sono coordinati e diretti dalla Commissione direttiva.

Art. 5. La Commissione direttiva
1. La Commissione programma e coordina le riunioni della Consulta. In relazione a quanto stabilito nel corso delle sedute ordinarie e straordinarie, si occupa della realizzazione dei progetti e delle iniziative promosse dalla Consulta, scegliendo a propria discrezione gli strumenti e le forme più idonee, in accordo con l'Amministrazione Comunale e in base alle risorse umane, economiche e strutturali a sua disposizione.
2. La Commissione è composta da due membri elettivi e due membri di diritto. I membri di diritto sono:
a) il Presidente, che è, di diritto, il Presidente della v Commissione Consiliare o suo delegato. Egli è garante della laicità e del carattere istituzionale di questo organismo;
b) il Direttore/Responsabile del Centro di In-Formazione Religiosa
[...]
c) il Segretario, che viene eletto a maggioranza dall'Assemblea
[...]
d) il Coordinatore che viene eletto a maggioranza dall'Assemblea, svolge un ruolo di moderatore, richiamandosi ai principi di rispetto delle diversità confessionali e valorizzazione del contributo umano, sociale e culturale che ogni comunità religiosa può apportare. Come membro della Commissione direttiva si occupa di armonizzare le attività del Centro nel quadro più organico delle attività culturali, sociali e formative del Comune di Firenze.

Art. 6. *Rappresentanza*
1. Ogni confessione religiosa interessata a far parte della Consulta deve indicare, con lettera formale di accreditamento, il nominativo di 1 rappresentante. Ogni rappresentante è chiamato, attraverso una partecipazione costante e responsabile, a contribuire con i valori culturali della propria fede allo studio e sviluppo di proposte e progetti della Consulta. La durata di ogni mandato di rappresentanza è a discrezione della propria confessione.
2. Qualora il rappresentante si rendesse responsabile di una condotta non consona ai principi operativi della Consulta, la Commissione direttiva è tenuta ad informarne la direzione o i responsabili territoriali della confessione rappresentata perché possano procedere ad adeguati richiami o provvedimenti, compresa la possibilità di una sua sostituzione.

Art. 7. *Diritto di Voto*
1. Hanno diritto di voto i membri della Commissione direttiva e un rappresentante per ogni confessione religiosa.
2. Considerata la pluralità delle denominazioni confessionali, specialmente in ambito cristiano, al fine di perseguire un principio di equilibrio e proporzionalità in sede di voto tra le fedi facenti parte della Consulta, si stabilisce che vi sia un rappresentante con diritto di voto per le seguenti aree confessionali: 1) Chiesa Cattolica; 2) Chiese Evangelico-Protestanti; 3) Chiese Ortodosse; 4) Chiese Anglicano-Episcopali; 5) Comunità Ebraica; 6) Comunità Islamica; 7) Comunità Buddista; 8) Comunità Baha'i, indicato dai membri della Consulta afferenti alla stessa area confessionale.

Art. 9. *Scopi e attività*
1. Gli scopi della Consulta sono:
– promuovere le relazioni, nell'ambito delle istituzioni laiche cittadine, tra le differenti confessioni religiose presenti sul territorio comunale, al fine di favorirne la reciproca conoscenza ed il dialogo tra le comunità religiose e la società civile;
– diffondere la conoscenza del pensiero di ogni confessione religiosa circa i temi etici e morali posti dai continui sviluppi della scienza e della società contemporanea;
– organizzare, nel rispetto della libertà religiosa, incontri ed attività finalizzate al superamento dei pregiudizi e delle incomprensioni culturali che spesso rappresentano l'origine di tensioni e conflitti nella cittadinanza;
– suggerire all'Amministrazione locale, secondo quanto espresso sopra, interventi e strumenti idonei alla promozione di un clima di pacifica convivenza e solidarietà tra i cittadini;
– contribuire alla promozione sociale e culturale della città di Firenze e della sua popolazione, sostenendo iniziative di carattere informativo e formativo rivolte in particolar modo alle scuole (primarie e secondarie), attraverso lo strumento del Centro di In-Formazione Religiosa.

Art. 10. *Modalità di riunione*
1. Le sedute ordinarie della Consulta hanno periodicità mensile.
[...]

Art. 11. *Relazioni con enti, istituzioni o associazioni affini*
1. La Consulta promuove le relazioni e la collaborazione con enti, istituzioni o associazioni affini ai suoi principi fondatori e scopi istituzionali, siano essi di natura pubblica, privata o confessionale. Eventuali relazioni e collabora-

zioni dovranno comunque essere oggetto di discussione ed approvazione (a maggioranza assoluta) da parte dei membri della Consulta.

CHAPTER 5

Mosques and Prayer Houses

At the national level, there is no general statute concerning places of worship, their establishment and management. Some principle can be found in case law and in legislation on urban planning. First of all, Italy recognises the right of all religions to establish places of worship on the basis of the religious freedom right enshrined in Article 19 of the Constitution.[1] Secondly, the issue of places of worship is among the competences of Regions and local authorities. Article 117 of the Constitution (see ch. 1) gives the Regions the power to legislate over the management of their territory, including matters related to places of worship.[2] Other statutes—adopted since the 1970s, when the legislative and administrative powers of the Regions and local bodies were defined—provide that the administratively competent authorities on urban matters are the Regions and local entities (Art. 94.2 of legislative decree n. 112 of 1998[3]). Places of worship shall be established and protected by the local administrative authorities as places of public interest (*opere di urbanizzazione secondaria*) in accordance with Act n. 847 of 1964 (Art. 4, as amended by Art. 44 of Act 865/1971[4]) and Act n. 10 of 1977 (*legge 'Bucalossi'*). These provisions also created a fund for buildings of public interest (including places of worship) which can be financed by public money. More recently, these principles have been restated by decree of the President of Republic n. 380 of 2011 on urban planning (*Testo Unico Edilizia*).[5]

1 Constitutional Court, judgment n. 59 of 18 November 1958, available at http://www.olir.it/documenti/?documento=374 (last accessed 4 February 2015).

2 In judgment no. 303/2003, the Constitutional Court considered that city planning—although not explicitly listed—should be included in matters of 'territory management', which is among the state/Regions concurrent competences (Art. 117, par. 3 of the Constitution).

3 Decreto legislativo 31 marzo 1998, n. 112, *Conferimento di funzioni e compiti amministrativi dello Stato alle regioni ed agli enti locali, in attuazione del capo I della legge 15 marzo 1997, n. 59* (available at www.normattiva.it/uri-res/N2Ls?urn:nir:stato:decreto.legislativo:1998-03-31;112, last accessed 5 February 2015).

4 Art. 44 of Act n. 865 of 1971 amended Art. 4 of Act n. 847 of 29 September 1964 and included places of worship in the list of buildings of public interest. Art. 1 of Act n. 847/1964 established the rules on the funding of those buildings and some basic conditions for urban plans.

5 See Art. 16.8. D.p.r. n. 380 of 2001 is available at www.normattiva.it/uri-res/N2Ls?urn:nir:stato:decreto.del.presidente.della.repubblica:2001-06-06;380!vig=2015-02-05 (last accessed 5 February 2015).

As municipalities are responsible for the services of the city, including urban planning, it is for the city councils, when adopting city plans, to allocate areas for buildings of public interest and, among them, places of worship. Normally, areas are attributed to the religious groups that live and act in the city: a certain level of organisation and/or public recognition is required, but drawing a distinction between religious denominations with an agreement with the state (*intesa*) and those without such an agreement has been declared illegal by various courts' decisions.[6]

The right to establish places of worship and its implementation at the local level is often regulated by Regional Acts. Not every Region has adopted systematic regulation on this issue, and rules on places of worship are often included in the general regulation of urban planning; therefore, the situation of Muslim communities differs, depending on regional provisions and on the municipal management of building areas. For example, Act n. 29 of 1988 of the Abruzzo Region is specifically dedicated to the urban rules on places of worship and it establishes in detail the procedure for building new places of worship (request by the religious denominations, building plans, competences of the municipalities, rules on public funding, rules for the city plans). This Act was amended after judgment of the Constitutional Court n. 195 of 1993, providing that these rules shall apply to all religious denominations (including those without agreement with the state). Similar legislation exists, for example, in the Basilicata (regional Act n. 9 of 17 April 1987[7]), Calabria (regional Act n. 21 of 1990[8]), and Liguria (regional Act n. 4 of 1985[9]) Regions. In some cases, provisions on places of worship are included in legislation about urban planning: for example, an act of the Campania Region of 2010 creates a special fund for places of worship;[10] a particular provision of regional Act n. 24 of 1998 of the Lazio Region refers to the building of places of worship promoted by the consular authorities of foreign states for their fellow citizens.[11]

6 See judgments of the Constitutional Court n. 195 of 1993 (http://www.olir.it/documenti/?documento=378) and n. 346 of 2002 (http://www.olir.it/documenti/index.php?argomento=0&documento=891, both accessed 5 February 2015). Both declared illegitimate regional Acts that, regulating urban planning and places of worship, had established more favourable treatment for religions with *intesa*.

7 http://www.olir.it/documenti/?documento=1932 (last accessed 5 February 2015).

8 http://www.olir.it/documenti/?documento=1938 (last accessed 5 February 2015).

9 http://www.olir.it/documenti/?documento=4228 (last accessed 5 February 2015).

10 Regional act n. 2 of 21 January 2010 (available at http://www.olir.it/documenti/?documento=5451, last accessed 5 February 2015).

11 Art. 18bis of regional Act n. 24 of 6 July 1998, as amended by regional Act n. 41 of 2001 (see the text below).

Another interesting situation is that of the Lombardia Region: regional Act n. 12 of 2005 on urban planning mentions (at Art. 71) the protection of buildings of associations with religious purposes; it provides for the construction of new places of worship, according to city plans, referring to associations or recognised bodies. This Act (adopted after the judgment of the Constitutional Court declaring illegitimate discrimination between religions with *intesa* and those without[12]) has been modified by regional Act n. 2 of 2015 which establishes several pre-conditions for the building of new places of worship. These conditions—which are disputable, looking at Italian principles on religious freedom—include the duty for religious denominations to conclude an agreement with municipalities, and to take measures (at their expense) to provide for parking and other structures within the area of the building. The Act also states that for security reasons a system of video control of new places of worship will be planned. In April 2015, the government referred this to the Constitutional Court, requesting it to determine the constitutionality of that law.[13]

All provisions and principles here mentioned are not specifically related to mosques, but they are applicable to all places of worship, including the Islamic ones.

In a few municipalities, the building of Muslim places of worship has followed a specific procedure. For example in Colle Val d'Elsa (Siena) a special agreement was signed between the municipality and the local Muslim community for the building of one of the few mosques in Italy. In Milan the already mentioned register of religious associations (see sect. 1.4) has been created in order to make easier the identification of the city's Muslim groups that wish to build or maintain mosques or prayer houses. In 2014 a deliberation of the city government specified three areas where a new place of worship should be built, publishing an announcement calling for building projects to be presented by the communities listed in the register.[14]

---

12 Constitutional Court, judgment n. 346 of 8 July 2002 (available at http://www.olir.it/documenti/?documento=891, last accessed 6 February 2015). The same principle was stated in the abovementioned judgment of the Constitutional Court n. 195 of 1993.

13 The government's appeal (through the President of the Council of Ministers) is available at http://www.olir.it/documenti/?documento=6529 (last accessed 15 May 2015).

14 The text of the deliberation is available at http://www.olir.it/documenti/index.php?documento=6423; the announcement of December 2014 is available at http://www.olir.it/documenti/?documento=6443 (both accessed 5 February 2015). The announcement is public and (obviously) not reserved to Muslim communities; however, it refers to the associations listed in the register of the City of Milan, so Muslim groups may especially benefit from this.

In general, we can observe that specific problems have arisen with regard to Muslim communities. General principles in regional Acts or in municipal decisions are sometimes not sufficient to proceed with the building of mosques, and some cases have been the subject of litigation.

Case Law

The general principle, stated by the Constitutional Court, is that the right to establish prayer houses is a part of the right to freedom of religion, and thus there is no need for an agreement (*intesa*) before this right can be enjoyed. The Constitutional Court annulled the provisions of the regional Acts of Lombardia and Abruzzo, which established that only religions with *intesa* could proceed to build new places of worship, or that public funds could not be allocated to religions without *intesa* (Regions, indeed, can provide resources for building new prayer houses and for the restoration of existing places).[15]

Regional acts and municipal administrative practice often require compliance with standards or procedures that Islamic communities can observe only with great difficulty, usually because the Muslim community does not have the required organisational structures, nor bodies with legal personality. A decision of the Administrative Regional Tribunal (TAR) of Lombardia of 28 December 2013 specified that the municipal authorities must take into account the presence of different religions in the city area. To this end, the lack of an agreement between the municipality and the local Muslim organisation cannot be the reason for denying the assignment of areas for mosques in the city plan: the signature of a protocol of agreement shall facilitate access to public funds, but shall not be a limit to the implementation of religious rights.[16]

Many cases have concerned building permits and, in particular, requests to rezone property for a religious use. This is a very common problem for Muslim groups, as they usually gather to pray in flats, basements, ex-storehouses, etc. Case law is diversified, depending on the degree of control exercised over compliance with specific urban rules. Frequently, cases have dealt with the lack of correspondence between the scopes and activities of Muslim associations

15 Constitutional Court, judgment n. 195 of 1993 on the Act of the Abruzzo Region (available at http://www.olir.it/documenti/?documento=378) and n. 346 of 2002 on the Act of the Lombardia Region (http://www.olir.it/documenti/?documento=891, both accessed 4 February 2015).

16 Decision n. 1176 of 28 December 2013, of the TAR section of Brescia, available at http://www.olir.it/documenti/?documento=6226 (last accessed 4 February 2015).

(which are often cultural associations) and the building or rezoning permits required for religious purposes. Normally tribunals have strictly applied local urban rules (among many others: TAR Lombardia, decision of 28 December 2009, n. 6226[17] and, on appeal, Council of State, decision of 27 November 2010 n. 8298[18]), without a specific analysis of the peculiar characteristics of the Muslim groups.[19]

An interesting court decision—connected to the problem of building or maintaining a prayer house—dealt with a municipal ordinance that prohibited the use of languages other than Italian in public gatherings and manifestations. The judge considered this ordinance to be discriminatory and illegitimate, because it could have the effect of limiting the exercise of freedom of association with religious purposes for those religious groups (like Islam) that do not gather in a proper place of worship (Tribunal of Brescia, ordinance n. 71 of 29 January 2010;[20] judgment of TAR Lombardia n. 19 of 15 January 2010[21]).

Regione Abruzzo. Legge Regionale 16 marzo 1988, n. 29. *Disciplina urbanistica dei servizi religiosi.*[22]

Art. 1

1. La presente legge regionale disciplina i rapporti intercorrenti tra insediamenti residenziali e servizi religiosi ad essi pertinenti, nel quadro delle attribuzioni spettanti rispettivamente ai Comuni ed agli enti istituzionalmente competenti in materia di culto della Chiesa Cattolica e delle altre confessioni

17 http://www.olir.it/documenti/?documento=5639 (last accessed 4 February 2015).

18 http://www.olir.it/documenti/?documento=5547 (last accessed 4 February 2015).

19 For example, the verification of rezoning requests has considered (among other aspects) the aim of the applying body, that it was a "cultural" and not a religious association, thus confirming the invalidity of the request. The overlapping cultural and religious aims of Muslim organisations are very common in Italy. See for example the decision of the Administrative Regional Tribunal (TAR) of Lombardia, of 22 September 2011 (at http://www.olir.it/documenti/?documento=5701, last accessed 4 February 2015).

20 http://www.olir.it/documenti/?documento=5249 (last accessed 4 February 2015).

21 http://www.olir.it/documenti/?documento=5247 (last accessed 4 February 2015).

22 The text, as amended by the judgment of the Constitutional Court and by subsequent regional Act n. 74 of 2001 and 72 of 1998, is available at http://www2.consiglio.regione.abruzzo.it/leggi_tv/testi_vigenti/insieme.asp?numero=29&anno=1988&lr=L.R.%2016%20marzo%201988,%20n.%2029&passo=../abruzzo_lr/1988/lr88029.htm&passa=http://leggi.regione.abruzzo.it/leggireg/1988/l029.htm&passa1=http://leggi.regione.abruzzo.it/leggireg/1988/l029.html (last accessed 2 February 2015).

religiose che abbiano una presenza organizzata nell'ambito dei Comuni interessati dalle previsioni urbanistiche di cui ai successivi articoli.
2. In mancanza dell'intesa prevista dal comma 3° dell'art. 8 della Costituzione, la natura di confessione religiosa potrà risultare anche da precedenti riconoscimenti pubblici, dallo statuto che ne esprima chiaramente i caratteri, o comunque dalla comune considerazione.

Art. 2
1. Ai sensi e per gli effetti dell'art. 3, 2° comma lettera b) del D.M. 2 aprile 1968 del Ministro dei lavori pubblici, sono attrezzature di interesse comune di tipo religioso:
a) gli immobili destinati al culto anche se articolati in più edifici;
b) gli immobili destinati all'abitazione dei ministri di culto;
c) gli immobili adibiti nell'esercizio del ministero pastorale, ad attività educative, culturali, sociali e ricreative, che non abbiano fini di lucro.
2. In relazione al disposto dell'art. 4 della legge 29 settembre 1964, n. 847 e successive modificazioni, le attrezzature di cui al precedente comma costituiscono opere di urbanizzazione secondaria ad ogni effetto.

Art. 3
1. In sede di formazione o di revisione degli strumenti urbanistici generali, i Comuni assicurano una dotazione di aree per abitante sino ad un massimo del 20% di quelle obbligatoriamente previste per attrezzature di interesse comune, specificatamente riservate ai servizi religiosi.
2. Nelle zone omogenee di tipo A e B, di cui al decreto del Ministro dei lavori pubblici 2 aprile 1968, le aree destinate ad attrezzature di tipo religioso sono computabili, ai fini della determinazione delle quantità minime prescritte dallo stesso decreto, in misura doppia di quella effettiva.
3. Le previsioni di nuovi servizi religiosi nell'ambito delle zone omogenee di tipo C di cui al decreto del Ministro dei lavori pubblici 2 aprile 1968, dovranno assicurare una superficie minima di mq 2000 per ogni insediamento ferme restando le entità minime di rapporti previste per gli altri servizi di interesse comune.
4. Le localizzazioni delle aree riservate alle attrezzature di tipo religioso sono effettuate sentiti i pareri delle competenti autorità religiose, riconosciute a norma di legge, ove ricorrano i requisiti di cui al precedente art. 1.
5. In sede di attuazione dello strumento urbanistico generale le aree destinate alle attività di cui ai precedenti commi sono ripartite tra le varie confessioni religiose, che abbiano i requisiti indicati all'art. 1, proporzionalmente alla loro consistenza, mediante concessione a titolo gratuito del diritto di superficie.

Art. 4
Qualora gli strumenti urbanistici generali vigenti non risultino conformi alle prescrizioni della presente legge, il Comune, di propria iniziativa, od entro sei mesi dalle eventuali richieste delle competenti autorità religiose, ne adegua le previsioni secondo le procedure ed i criteri di cui al precedente art. 3.
La relativa variante allo strumento urbanistico generale, ove vengano prescelte aree già destinate da questo a servizi pubblici, è definitivamente approvata con deliberazione del Consiglio comunale non soggetta alla pubblicazione di cui all'art. 9 della legge 17 agosto 1942, n. 1150 e successive modificazioni; negli altri casi la variante segue l'ordinario procedimento di formazione previsto di tale legge.

Art. 5
1. I Comuni devolvono entro il 31 marzo di ogni anno alle competenti autorità religiose di cui alla presente legge una aliquota pari al 10 % dei contributi per urbanizzazione secondaria loro dovuti.
2. I contributi di cui al precedente comma sono determinati avuto riguardo a tutte le concessioni edilizie onerose rilasciate nell'anno precedente, anche relativamente all'edilizia convenzionata, senza tener conto degli scomputi che i titolari delle concessioni abbiano eventualmente ottenuto per l'esecuzione diretta delle opere di urbanizzazione secondaria e per cessione delle relative aree.
3. I contributi sono corrisposti alle confessioni religiose che presentino apposita richiesta, entro il 31 dicembre di ciascun anno, al Sindaco del Comune interessato e che abbiano i requisiti di cui al precedente comma 1, proporzionalmente alla loro diffusione sul territorio ed alla loro incidenza sociale.
4. Le richieste non necessitano degli elaborati progettuali in allegato, dovendo i beneficiari ottemperare a quanto disposto dall'art. 6, comma 1.
5. Le richieste di cui al precedente comma 3 vengono presentate dai singoli ministri di culto operanti nel territorio comunale, o da uno di essi, in nome e per conto di tutti gli altri.
6. I contributi di cui al comma 1 sono erogati dai Comuni in favore dell'autorità esponenziale della confessione religiosa, la quale provvede alla ripartizione degli stessi tra i singoli ministeri di culto che ne hanno fatto richiesta ai sensi del precedente comma 4.

Art. 5-bis
1. Ai fini della devoluzione dei contributi di cui all'art. 5 comma 1, l'Ufficio di Ragioneria di ogni Comune della Regione, su ciascuna reversale di incasso relativa ai contributi per urbanizzazione secondaria, storna una percentuale

pari al 10% dell'importo introitato e lo destina ad un sotto conto corrente vincolato appositamente costituito presso la tesoreria del Comune, il quale può essere utilizzato unicamente per la corresponsione di quanto dovuto alle autorità religiose.
2. Entro il 15 aprile di ogni anno, i comuni fanno pervenire all'Assessorato Regionale ai Lavori Pubblici un dettagliato resoconto, da cui risulti che la devoluzione dei contributi per l'urbanizzazione secondaria alle autorità religiose è avvenuta nel pieno rispetto dei termini e dell'aliquota di cui all'art. 5 comma 1.
[...]

Art. 6
1. I contributi, entro tre anni dal loro versamento, sono utilizzati per la realizzazione e ristrutturazione delle attrezzature di cui al precedente art. 2; a tal fine le competenti autorità religiose trasmettono ai comuni, entro il 31 dicembre di ogni anno, un'analitica relazione sull'utilizzazione delle somme percepite e già utilizzate per le finalità della presente legge.
2. È in facoltà delle competenti autorità religiose di regolare i rapporti con il Comune attraverso apposite convenzioni nel caso in cui il Comune stesso o i soggetti attuatori di piani urbanistici esecutivi provvedano alla realizzazione diretta dei lavori o delle opere di cui al precedente art. 2.
3. Le somme non utilizzate sono recuperate dal Comune maggiorate degli interessi computati al tasso riconosciuto dal tesoriere per le giacenze ordinarie.

Art. 7
1. L'amministrazione regionale, sentita la competente autorità ecclesiastica, è autorizzata a concedere contributi per la ristrutturazione, consolidamento, ampliamento e straordinaria manutenzione di edifici destinati al culto, di immobili adibiti nell'esercizio pastorale ad attività educative, culturali, sociali e ricreative che non abbiano fini di lucro nonché per l'ammodernamento, il restauro e la conservazione di arredi, impianti ed opere artistiche.
2. I contributi di cui al comma precedente possono essere erogati anche per lavori da compiersi all'abitazione dei ministri del culto e del personale che presta servizio agli edifici di culto.
3. Le previste contribuzioni hanno carattere integrativo e possono anche essere concesse ad opere che fruiscono di contributi statali.
[...]

Regione Lazio, legge regionale n. 24, 6 Luglio 1998. ***Pianificazione paesistica e tutela dei beni e delle aree sottoposti a vincolo paesistico***[23]

Art. 18 bis *Sedi di rappresentanza diplomatica e consolare*
1. Qualora nell'ambito di aree soggette a disciplina di tutela integrale o ad essa assimilata, previste dai PTP, ivi compresi quelli approvati con deliberazione del Consiglio regionale antecedente alla data di entrata in vigore della presente legge, o dal PTPR, ricadono sedi di rappresentanza diplomatica e consolare in ordine alle quali siano in essere o vengano definiti accordi bilaterali in regime di reciprocità tra lo Stato italiano ed altri Stati, è consentita, in deroga alla citata disciplina di tutela, la costruzione di edifici autonomi da destinare ad attività di culto per il soddisfacimento delle esigenze della comunità.
2. Nei casi previsti dal comma 1 i progetti delle opere sono corredati del SIP di cui agli articoli 29 e 30.

Regione Lombardia. Legge regionale 11 marzo 2005, n. 12. ***Legge per il governo del territorio***[24]

CAPO III. Norme per la Realizzazione di Edifici di culto e di attrezzature destinate a Servizi Religiosi

Art. 70. *Finalità.*
1. La Regione ed i comuni concorrono a promuovere, conformemente ai criteri di cui al presente capo, la realizzazione di attrezzature di interesse comune destinate a servizi religiosi da effettuarsi da parte degli enti istituzionalmente competenti in materia di culto della Chiesa Cattolica.
2. Le disposizioni del presente capo si applicano anche agli enti delle altre confessioni religiose con le quali lo Stato ha già approvato con legge la relativa intesa ai sensi dell'articolo 8, terzo comma, della Costituzione.
2 bis. Le disposizioni del presente capo si applicano altresì agli enti delle altre confessioni religiose che presentano i seguenti requisiti:

23 The text, amended by regional act n. 41 of 2001, is available at http://www.consiglio.regione.lazio.it/consiglioweb/leggi_regionali.php#.VNXz1vmG-So (last accessed 5 February 2015).

24 The text, as amended by regional act n. 2 of 3 February 2015, is available at http://normelombardia.consiglio.regione.lombardia.it/NormeLombardia/Accessibile/main.aspx?view=showdoc&selnode=0&iddoc=lr002005031100012 (last accessed 7 February 2015).

a) presenza diffusa, organizzata e consistente a livello territoriale e un significativo insediamento nell'ambito del comune nel quale vengono effettuati gli interventi disciplinati dal presente capo;
b) i relativi statuti esprimono il carattere religioso delle loro finalità istituzionali e il rispetto dei principi e dei valori della Costituzione.
2 ter. Ai fini dell'applicazione delle disposizioni del presente capo gli enti delle confessioni religiose di cui ai commi 2 e 2 bis devono stipulare una convenzione a fini urbanistici con il comune interessato. Le convenzioni prevedono espressamente la possibilità della risoluzione o della revoca, in caso di accertamento da parte del comune di attività non previste nella convenzione.
2 quater. Per consentire ai comuni la corretta applicazione delle disposizioni di cui al presente capo, viene istituita e nominata con provvedimento di Giunta regionale, che stabilisce anche composizione e modalità di funzionamento, una consulta regionale per il rilascio di parere preventivo e obbligatorio sulla sussistenza dei requisiti di cui al comma 2 bis. La consulta opera senza oneri aggiuntivi a carico del bilancio regionale.
3. I contributi e le provvidenze disciplinati dalla presente legge hanno natura distinta ed integrativa rispetto ai finanziamenti a favore dell'edilizia di culto previsti in altre leggi dello Stato e della Regione, nonché in atti o provvedimenti amministrativi dei comuni diretti a soddisfare specifici interessi locali nell'esercizio delle proprie funzioni istituzionali.

Art. 71.*Ambito di applicazione*
1. Sono attrezzature di interesse comune per servizi religiosi:
a) gli immobili destinati al culto anche se articolati in più edifici compresa l'area destinata a sagrato;
b) gli immobili destinati all'abitazione dei ministri del culto, del personale di servizio, nonché quelli destinati ad attività di formazione religiosa;
c) nell'esercizio del ministero pastorale, gli immobili adibiti ad attività educative, culturali, sociali, ricreative e di ristoro compresi gli immobili e le attrezzature fisse destinate alle attività di oratorio e similari che non abbiano fini di lucro;
c bis) gli immobili destinati a sedi di associazioni, società o comunità di persone in qualsiasi forma costituite, le cui finalità statutarie o aggregative siano da ricondurre alla religione, all'esercizio del culto o alla professione religiosa quali sale di preghiera, scuole di religione o centri culturali.
2. Le attrezzature di cui al comma 1 costituiscono opere di urbanizzazione secondaria ad ogni effetto, a norma dell'articolo 44, comma 4.
3. Gli edifici di culto e le attrezzature di interesse comune per servizi religiosi interamente costruiti con i contributi di cui al presente capo non pos-

sono essere in ogni caso sottratti alla loro destinazione, che deve risultare trascritta con apposito atto nei registri immobiliari, se non siano decorsi almeno vent'anni dall'erogazione del contributo. Tale vincolo di destinazione si estende anche agli edifici di culto ed alle altre attrezzature di interesse comune per servizi religiosi costruiti su aree cedute in diritto di superficie agli enti delle confessioni religiose che ne siano assegnatari i quali sono tenuti al rimborso dei contributi ed alla restituzione delle aree in caso di mutamento della destinazione d'uso delle attrezzature costruite sulle predette aree.

Art. 72. *Piano per le attrezzature religiose*
1. Le aree che accolgono attrezzature religiose o che sono destinate alle attrezzature stesse sono specificamente individuate nel piano delle attrezzature religiose, atto separato facente parte del piano dei servizi, dove vengono dimensionate e disciplinate sulla base delle esigenze locali, valutate le istanze avanzate dagli enti delle confessioni religiose di cui all'articolo 70.
2. L'installazione di nuove attrezzature religiose presuppone il piano di cui al comma 1; senza il suddetto piano non può essere installata nessuna nuova attrezzatura religiosa da confessioni di cui all'articolo 70.
3. Il piano di cui al comma 1è sottoposto alla medesima procedura di approvazione dei piani componenti il PGT di cui all'articolo 13.
4. Nel corso del procedimento per la predisposizione del piano di cui al comma 1 vengono acquisiti i pareri di organizzazioni, comitati di cittadini, esponenti e rappresentanti delle forze dell'ordine oltre agli uffici provinciali di questura e prefettura al fine di valutare possibili profili di sicurezza pubblica, fatta salva l'autonomia degli organi statali. Resta ferma la facoltà per i comuni di indire referendum nel rispetto delle previsioni statutarie e dell'ordinamento statale.
5. I comuni che intendono prevedere nuove attrezzature religiose sono tenuti ad adottare e approvare il piano delle attrezzature religiose entro diciotto mesi dalla data di entrata in vigore della legge regionale recante "Modifiche alla legge regionale 11 marzo 2005, n. 12 (Legge per il governo del territorio)— Principi per la pianificazione delle attrezzature per servizi religiosi". Decorso detto termine il piano è approvato unitamente al nuovo PGT.
6. Il piano delle attrezzature religiose può avere valenza sovracomunale, sulla base di una convenzione tra comuni limitrofi che individua il comune capofila. La procedura di cui all'articolo 4 deve avvenire singolarmente in ogni comune. Il provvedimento finale e conclusivo della procedura è unico e ne è responsabile il comune capofila. Il piano delle attrezzature religiose sovracomunale costituisce parte del piano dei servizi dei singoli comuni che hanno aderito alla convenzione di cui sopra.

7. Il piano delle attrezzature religiose deve prevedere tra l'altro:
a) la presenza di strade di collegamento adeguatamente dimensionate o, se assenti o inadeguate, ne prevede l'esecuzione o l'adeguamento con onere a carico dei richiedenti;
b) la presenza di adeguate opere di urbanizzazione primaria o, se assenti o inadeguate, ne prevede l'esecuzione o l'adeguamento con onere a carico dei richiedenti;
c) distanze adeguate tra le aree e gli edifici da destinare alle diverse confessioni religiose. Le distanze minime sono definite con deliberazione della Giunta regionale;
d) uno spazio da destinare a parcheggio pubblico in misura non inferiore al 200 per cento della superficie lorda di pavimento dell'edificio da destinare a luogo di culto. Il piano dei servizi può prevedere in aggiunta un minimo di posteggi determinati su coefficienti di superficie convenzionali;
e) la realizzazione di un impianto di videosorveglianza esterno all'edificio, con onere a carico dei richiedenti, che ne monitori ogni punto di ingresso, collegato con gli uffici della polizia locale o forze dell'ordine;
f) la realizzazione di adeguati servizi igienici, nonché l'accessibilità alle strutture anche da parte di disabili;
g) la congruità architettonica e dimensionale degli edifici di culto previsti con le caratteristiche generali e peculiari del paesaggio lombardo, così come individuate nel PTR.
8. Le disposizioni del presente articolo non si applicano alle attrezzature religiose esistenti alla entrata in vigore della legge recante "Modifiche alla legge regionale 11 marzo 2005, n. 12 (Legge per il governo del territorio)—Principi per la pianificazione delle attrezzature per servizi religiosi"[25].

Art. 73. *Modalità e procedure di finanziamento*
1. In ciascun comune, almeno l'8 per cento delle somme riscosse per oneri di urbanizzazione secondaria è ogni anno accantonato in apposito fondo, risultante in modo specifico nel bilancio di previsione, destinato alla realizzazione delle attrezzature indicate all'articolo 71, nonché per interventi manutentivi, di restauro e ristrutturazione edilizia, ampliamento e dotazione di impianti, ovvero all'acquisto delle aree necessarie. Tale fondo è determinato

25 This provision refers to regional Act n. 2 of 3 February 2015 (available at http://www.olir.it/documenti/index.php?argomento=0&documento=6468, last accessed 7 February 2015), providing that rules on video control and other pre-requisites for new places of worship shall not apply to existing religious buildings.

con riguardo a tutti i permessi di costruire rilasciati e alle denunce di inizio attività presentate nell'anno precedente in relazione a interventi a titolo oneroso ed è incrementato di una quota non inferiore all'8 per cento:
a) del valore delle opere di urbanizzazione realizzate direttamente dai soggetti interessati a scomputo totale o parziale del contributo relativo agli oneri di urbanizzazione secondaria;
b) del valore delle aree cedute per la realizzazione delle opere di urbanizzazione secondaria;
c) di ogni altro provento destinato per legge o per atto amministrativo alla realizzazione di opere di urbanizzazione secondaria.
2. I contributi sono corrisposti agli enti delle confessioni religiose di cui all'articolo 70 che ne facciano richiesta. A tal fine le autorità religiose competenti, secondo l'ordinamento proprio di ciascuna confessione, presentano al comune entro il 30 giugno di ogni anno un programma di massima, anche pluriennale, degli interventi da effettuare, dando priorità alle opere di restauro e di risanamento conservativo del proprio patrimonio architettonico esistente, corredato dalle relative previsioni di spesa.
3. Entro il successivo 30 novembre, il comune, dopo aver verificato che gli interventi previsti nei programmi presentati rientrino tra quelli di cui all'articolo 71, comma 1, ripartisce i predetti contributi tra gli enti di cui all'articolo 70 che ne abbiano fatto istanza, tenuto conto della consistenza ed incidenza sociale nel comune delle rispettive confessioni religiose, finanziando in tutto o in parte i programmi a tal fine presentati. Tali contributi, da corrispondere entro trenta giorni dall'esecutività della deliberazione di approvazione del bilancio annuale di previsione, sono utilizzati entro tre anni dalla loro assegnazione e la relativa spesa documentata con relazione che gli enti assegnatari trasmettono al comune entro sei mesi dalla conclusione dei lavori.
4. È in facoltà delle competenti autorità religiose di regolare i rapporti con il comune attraverso convenzioni nel caso in cui il comune stesso od i soggetti attuatori di piani urbanistici provvedano alla realizzazione diretta delle attrezzature di cui all'articolo 71.
5. Nel caso in cui non siano presentate istanze ai sensi del comma 2, l'ammontare del fondo è utilizzato per altre opere di urbanizzazione.

Protocollo di intesa tra il Comune di Colle di Val D'Elsa e l'Associazione "Comunità dei Musulmani di Siena e Provincia" con sede in Colle di Val d'Elsa. 30 dicembre 2004[26]

Il Comune di Colle di Val d'Elsa e l'Associazione "Comunità dei Musulmani di Siena e Provincia" con sede in Colle di Val d'Elsa,

CONSIDERATO che la Costituzione riconosce i diritti fondamentali della persona umana e le libertà di pensiero, di coscienza e di religione
[…]

CONSIDERATO che in forza dell'articolo 8, secondo e terzo comma, della Costituzione le confessioni religiose, diverse da quella cattolica, hanno diritto di organizzarsi secondo i propri statuti, in quanto non contrastino con l'ordinamento giuridico italiano, e che i loro rapporti con lo Stato sono regolati per legge sulla base d'intese con le relative rappresentanze,

TENUTO CONTO che in occasione della realizzazione di un Centro Culturale a Colle di Val d'Elsa la stipula di un preventivo Protocollo d'Intesa appare atto di altissimo profilo etico e politico al fine di conseguire l'obiettivo comune dell'accoglienza, dell'integrazione e della solidarietà all'interno di un'unica società civile fondata oltre che sul perseguimento del benessere comune e sul lavoro, principalmente sulla pace, sulla tolleranza e sul reciproco rispetto umano;

RICONOSCIUTA l'opportunità di addivenire al presente Protocollo, entrambe le parti convengono che le disposizioni seguenti rappresentino una prima intesa locale tra il Comune di Colle di Val D'Elsa e l'Associazione "Comunità dei Musulmani di Siena e Provincia" con sede in Colle di Val d'Elsa (di seguito denominata per brevità "Associazione") funzionale alla realizzazione, su questo territorio comunale, di un Centro Culturale Islamico, e annessa sala di preghiera per l'esercizio del relativo culto, a dimostrazione e testimonianza del reciproco desiderio di approfondimento della conoscenza e del rispetto avente quale unico fondamento il desiderio bilaterale di un dialogo su basi paritarie.

26 http://www.olir.it/documenti/?documento=1734 (last accessed 5 February 2015).

TENUTO CONTO che in conformità ai principi della Costituzione Italiana, è riconosciuto il diritto di professare e praticare liberamente ogni religione, compresa quella islamica, sia in forma individuale che associata, di farne propaganda e di esercitarne in privato o in pubblico il culto e i riti.

RILEVATA la necessità di garantire anche ai praticanti la religione islamica presenti sul territorio comunale, alle loro associazioni e organizzazioni e alle Comunità musulmane presenti la piena libertà di riunione e di manifestazione del pensiero con la parola e Io scritto e ogni altro mezzo di diffusione.

Art. 1. (Libertà religiosa)
Il Comune di Colle di Val D'Elsa si impegna a riconoscere e favorire sul proprio territorio la parità di tutela del sentimento religioso e dei diritti di libertà religiosa, senza discriminazioni tra i cittadini e tra i culti.
Il Comune di Colle di Val D'Elsa si appella al disposto dell'articolo 3 della Legge 13 ottobre 1975, n. 654, per le manifestazioni di intolleranza e pregiudizio religioso.

Art. 2. (Edifici di culto)
L'edificio destinato all'esercizio pubblico del culto islamico situato sull'area di proprietà del Comune di Colle di Val D'Elsa, non può essere sottratto alla sua destinazione neppure per effetto di alienazione, fino a che la destinazione stessa non sia cessata con il consenso del Comune stesso.
Tale edificio non può essere requisito, occupato, espropriato o demolito se non per gravi ed urgenti ragioni di pubblica utilità. Le parti precisano riconoscono e ribadiscono che le aree concesse dal Comune di Colle di Val D'Elsa in diritto di superficie all'Associazione per la realizzazione del Centro Culturale, oltre che tutte le opere strutturali ed infrastrutturali sulla stessa realizzate, sono e rimarranno, per tutta la durata della concessione, di esclusivo uso pubblico e, compatibilmente con la pratica religiosa, sono sempre accessibili da parte di chiunque vi abbia interesse, quale punto di riferimento e di dialogo tra culture e religioni.

Art. 3. (Albo delle Associazioni di Volontariato e di Promozione sociale)
L'Associazione, costituita in conformità delle norme del Codice civile, è tenuta ad iscriversi in apposito registro tenuto presso il Comune di Colle di Val D'Elsa. L'iscrizione dovrà recare la sede, il cognome e nome degli amministratori dell'Associazione con la menzione di quelli ai quali è attribuita la rappresentanza.

L'iscrizione nel suddetto Registro è la condizione per il riconoscimento di benefici e vantaggi da parte del Comune di Colle di Val D'Elsa.

Art. 4. (Comitato Scientifico di Garanzia)
La gestione ordinaria e gli atti di straordinaria amministrazione relativi al Centro Culturale si svolgono sotto la soprintendenza ed il coordinamento di un Comitato Scientifico di Garanzia, organo paritetico composto da otto membri di cui quattro nominati dal Sindaco di Colle di Val D'Elsa ed i restanti dall'Organo di gestione dell'Associazione, tutti scelti fra persone di comprovata esperienza nelle tematiche culturali e religiose, assicurando, ove possibile, la presenza di ambo i sessi nel suddetto Organo.
Il Comitato Scientifico di Garanzia elegge a maggioranza al proprio interno un Presidente con funzioni di rappresentanza e di coordinamento dei lavori.
Il Comitato scientifico dura in carica tre anni a decorrere dalla data di stipula del presente Protocollo.
I membri sono rieleggibili.
L'assenza a più di tre sedute senza giustificati motivi comporta la decadenza dalla nomina con facoltà per i soggetti competenti di provvedere alla loro cooptazione.

Art. 5 (Attività del Centro Culturale)
Il Comitato Scientifico Paritetico di Garanzia ha i seguenti compiti:
– collabora con l'organo esecutivo dell'associazione per la predisposizione del Programma annuale delle "attività diverse" da svolgere all'interno del Centro Culturale, in funzione degli indirizzi generali del presente protocollo d'intesa e lo trasmette all'Amministrazione Comunale;
– verifica l'attuazione del Programma e relaziona periodicamente all'Amministrazione Comunale sull'attività del Centro Culturale;
– rappresenta il "punto d'ascolto" di tutti i cittadini sulle diverse problematiche, presenti e future, interessanti le tematiche del multireligioso e del multietnico;
– promuove attività, iniziative, incontri, tesi all'integrazione e al dialogo multiculturale e multireligioso a favore dell'intera comunità;
– garantisce il profilo scientifico di eventuali convegni, seminari, forum, dibattiti eventualmente promossi e realizzati nel Centro Culturale.
Tutte le attività del Centro Culturale sono aperte al pubblico nel rispetto dei principi del presente Protocollo d'Intesa e in particolare di quelli religiosi del culto islamico.
[...]

Gli atti di pertinenza dell'Associazione, l'affissione e la distribuzione di pubblicazioni e stampati di carattere religioso all'interno e all'ingresso dei luoghi di culto nonché delle sedi del Centro Culturale e le raccolte di fondi ivi eseguite sono liberi e non soggetti ad oneri.

Art. 6. (Regime tributario)
Agli effetti tributari l'Associazione avente fine di religione o di culto, come pure le attività dirette a tali scopi sono equiparati a quelli aventi fini di beneficenza o di istruzione.
Tali enti hanno il diritto di svolgere liberamente attività diverse da quelle di religione o di culto che restano, però, soggette alle leggi dello Stato concernenti tali attività e al regime tributario previsto per le medesime.
Qualora l'Associazione sia stata costituita nella forma di Organizzazione Non Lucrativa di Utilità Sociale (ONLUS) ai sensi del D. Lgs. 4 dicembre 1997, n. 460, si obbliga a rispettarne interamente i contenuti per il mantenimento del regime fiscale agevolativi.

Art. 7. (Ulteriori intese)
Le parti sottoporranno a nuovo esame il contenuto della presente intesa al termine del terzo anno dalla data di sottoscrizione della presente.
[…]

Art. 8. (Lingua)
L'Associazione si obbliga ad adottare, all'interno delle aree concesse in diritto di superficie, la lingua italiana, fatta eccezione per particolari attività di rito e di culto.

Art. 9. (Clausola Risolutiva espressa e mantenimento vincolo di destinazione)
Il Comune di Colle di Val D'Elsa assicura e riconosce, per tutta la durata di efficacia del contratto di concessione in diritto di superficie delle aree di proprietà comunale ove insisterà il Centro Culturale, la destinazione di tutti i detti spazi ivi realizzati anche a luogo di preghiera e di professione della fede islamica.
La violazione di una soltanto delle prescrizioni espresse nel presente Protocollo d'Intesa, così come pure in caso di eventuali condanne penali a carico dei componenti dell'organo direttivo dell'Associazione per aver commesso, direttamente o anche soltanto indirettamente, attività illegali legate alle attività svolte nel Centro Culturale, saranno valutate dalla Giunta Comunale quale possibile motivo di risoluzione di ogni contratto in essere fra il Comune di Colle di Val D'Elsa e l'Associazione, con particolare riferimento a quello

inerente il diritto di superficie dell'area di proprietà comunale per la realizzazione del Centro Culturale. Anche nel caso suddetto il Comune assicura tuttavia il mantenimento del vincolo di destinazione d'uso del Centro Culturale quale luogo ove esercitare anche il culto e la pratica della religione dell'islam, per un periodo non inferiore a trenta anni.

In caso di risoluzione del contratto di concessione, tutti i beni immobili realizzati al di sopra e al di sotto delle aree concesse, seppur con il permanere del vincolo di destinazione espresso al precedente comma, sono acquisiti di diritto al patrimonio del Comune di Colle di Val D'Elsa senza diritto a rivalsa, a risarcimenti di sorta, a restituzioni o a rimborsi avanzati da chiunque ed a qualsiasi titolo.

CHAPTER 6

Burial and Cemeteries

Italian legislation on burial and cemeteries does not make explicit reference to religious aspects, except for Article 100 of decree of the President of the Republic n. 285 of 1990 regulating cemeteries and burial policy. All cemeteries are regulated at the municipal level, in accordance with the decree of 1990; normally burial procedures do not refer to religion, even if many practices follow the Catholic tradition (the use of a coffin, ordinary methods of burial through inhumation, etc.). Article 100, par. 1, of d.p.r. n. 285/1990 states that the municipal plans on cemeteries can establish special sections for non-Catholics. Paragraph 2 permits separate sections to be reserved also for foreign residents in the town.[1] The organisation of these sections is within the competence of the local authorities.

Some regulations issued by municipalities take into account the right of all religions to perform funeral rites in their places of worship and according to their convictions, as well as the possibility of establishing special sections in the cemetery plans of the city. For example, a 2002 regulation of the city of Modena establishes that there should be a special Islamic section in the cemetery and that burial according to Muslim rules is permitted, including the possibility of the burial of bodies in a shroud.[2] In some cases, special sections

1 A circular of the Ministry of Health, explaining d.p.r. n. 285/1990, specified that for non-Catholics burial without a coffin (wrapping the body in a sheet) is legitimate. The text of the circular is available at http://www.gazzettaufficiale.it/eli/id/1998/08/19/098A7431/sg (last accessed 26 January 2015).

2 Other examples, not published here: Regulation on mortuary policy of the City of Milano, 18 January 2015 (Articles 13 and 14, available at http://www.olir.it/documenti/?documento=6478, last accessed 6 January 2016); Regulation of the City of Turin on mortuary policy, approved with deliberation of the City Council of 11 October 1999, and subsequent amendments (Art. 31, available at http://www.comune.torino.it/regolamenti/264/264.htm, last accessed 26 January 2015); deliberation of the City Council of Biella, n. 201 of 6 April 2010 (available at http://www.comune.biella.it/sito/file/biellaonline/delibere_giunta_comunale/2010/delgc201.pdf, last accessed 26 January 2015); Deliberation of the City Council of Trento, approving the regulation on mortuary policy, n. 38 of 9 April 1997, Art. 32 (http://www.comune.trento.it/Aree-tematiche/Servizi-funerari-e-cimiteriali/Normativa/A15-Regolamento-comunale-di-polizia-mortuaria, last accessed 26 January 2015).

in the municipal cemetery have been established through agreements with the local Islamic community.[3]

Decreto del Presidente della Repubblica 10 settembre 1990, n. 285. ***Approvazione del regolamento di polizia mortuaria***[4]
(*GU n. 239 del 12-10-1990—Suppl. Ordinario n. 63*)

Art. 100
1. I piani regolatori cimiteriali di cui all'art. 54 possono prevedere reparti speciali e separati per la sepoltura di cadaveri di persone professanti un culto diverso da quello cattolico.
2. Alle comunità straniere, che fanno domanda di avere un reparto proprio per la sepoltura delle salme dei loro connazionali, può parimenti essere data dal sindaco in concessione un'area adeguata nel cimitero.

Comune di Modena. Regolamento comunale di polizia mortuaria, 9 settembre 2002[5]

Art. 4. *Ammissione nelle strutture cimiteriali*
Nei cimiteri, salvo sia richiesta altra destinazione, sono ricevute e seppellite, senza distinzione di origine, di cittadinanza o di religione, le salme e le ceneri di persone: a) decedute nel territorio del Comune di Modena; b) ovunque decedute, ma aventi nel Comune stesso, al momento della morte, la residenza; [...]

Art. 8. *Sepolture Cimitero Musulmano*
Per la sepoltura nel campo destinato all'inumazione delle salme di persone professanti la religione musulmana esistono due aree: una da destinarsi all'inumazione ordinaria a titolo oneroso l'altra, di pari estensione, com-

3 For example: agreement of 30 May 2012 between the municipality of Cremona and the Muslim community in Cremona, available at http://www.olir.it/documenti/?documento=6255 (last accessed 26 January 2015); a draft agreement has also been prepared between the municipality of Bolzano and the Islamic local community (available at http://www.comune.bolzano.it/UploadDocs/11323_cimiteroislamico_convenzioneita.pdf, last accessed 26 January 2015).

4 www.normattiva.it/uri-res/N2Ls?urn:nir:stato:decreto.del.presidente.della.repubblica:1990-09-10;285 (last accessed 26 January 2015).

5 http://www.comune.modena.it/il-comune/regolamenti/regolamenti-di-sicurezza-igiene-pubblica-e-uso-del-territorio/regolamento-comunale-di-polizia-mortuaria (last accessed 26 January 2015).

prende zone da destinarsi alla concessione in uso novantennale, a titolo oneroso, con applicazione della stessa tariffa prevista per il Cimitero ebraico nel Viale Centrale. Tali aree non possono essere concesse a viventi. E' necessario il parere della Comunità Musulmana prima di procedere alla sepoltura.

Art. 10. *Inumazioni in reparti speciali entro i cimiteri*
Nei reparti speciali previsti dall'art. 100 del D.P.R. n. 285/90 per la sepoltura di persone di culto diverso da quello cattolico, per i culti religiosi che lo prevedano espressamente è consentita, come indicato anche dalla circ. Min. Sanità n. 10/98, la inumazione del cadavere avvolto unicamente in un lenzuolo di cotone. Per il trasporto funebre è d'obbligo l'uso della cassa di legno o, nei casi stabiliti, la duplice cassa di legno e zinco.

CHAPTER 7

Education and Schools

The principles on education are laid down in the Italian Constitution: Article 33 sets out the principle of the freedom of education and the right of private individuals and organisations to set up private schools (see sect. 7.3); Article 34 refers to the state's duty to provide public education, free of charge and open to all, which is compulsory in the first school cycles (see sect. 7.1).

7.1 Compulsory Education

Article 34 of the Constitution states that everyone has the right to public and free education, and Article 33.2 gives the state the authority to regulate public education and to create schools; various acts and decrees have been approved, applying these principles, in order to organise the different school cycles. Legislation in force establishes that education is compulsory for 10 years, from 6 to 16 years of age, and it is organised in different cycles.[1] The compulsory cycles include the primary school (5 years), the lower secondary school (3 years) and the first two years of the upper secondary school.[2] After the lower secondary school, pupils can attend an upper secondary schools or a vocational or training course. The latter are organised under the responsibility of the Regions (law 133/2008).

---

1 The organisation of the education system is the result of a complex set of different legislative reforms. Amendments are frequent in this area; the main pieces of legislation are Act n. 53 of 28 March 2003 which redefined and broadened the concept of compulsory schooling and compulsory training, introducing the "right-duty" to education and training for at least 12 years from the age of 6 (later reduced to 10 years); this "right-duty" is fulfilled through the education system or vocational training. The details of this system were defined by Act no. 296 of 27 December 2006 (Financial law 2007); ministerial decree n. 139/2007; Act no. 133 of 6 August 2008; Act no. 169 of 30 October 2008 containing urgent measures on education and university.

2 A description of the Italian education system has been prepared by Italian EURYDICE Unit, Structures of Education and Training Systems in Europe, Italy 2009–2010, available at http://www.indire.it/lucabas/lkmw_file/eurydice///STRUTTURE_2009_2010_EN.pdf; see also the website of Eurydice, European network on Education (https://webgate.ec.europa.eu/fpfis/mwikis/eurydice/index.php?title=Italy:Overview&oldid=103231).

Compulsory education refers to both enrolment and attendance. It can be accomplished either in a state school or in a private educational institution, if recognised by the law (*scuola paritaria*, a school authorised by the state issuing certificates that are equivalent to the public). Under certain conditions, parental schooling and merely private schools are also permitted and can satisfy the requirement of compulsory education (Art. 111 of legislative decree n. 297 of 1994).[3] Parents or carers are responsible for the completion of the cycle of compulsory education; the supervision of its implementation is the responsibility of school directors and of local authorities where pupils live.[4]

Once compulsory schooling has been completed, pupils who do not pursue their studies receive a certification attesting to the fulfilment of compulsory education and the competences acquired; these latter constitute formative credits for the attainment of any professional qualification. As for private or parental education, pupils must pass an examination in order to get a certification, which is necessary for continuing to study in a state educational institution (for example to access upper secondary schools or university).[5]

Costituzione

Art. 33.
L'arte e la scienza sono libere e libero ne è l'insegnamento.
La Repubblica detta le norme generali sull'istruzione ed istituisce scuole statali per tutti gli ordini e gradi.
Enti e privati hanno il diritto di istituire scuole ed istituti di educazione, senza oneri per lo Stato.
La legge, nel fissare i diritti e gli obblighi delle scuole non statali che chiedono la parità, deve assicurare ad esse piena libertà e ai loro alunni un trattamento scolastico equipollente a quello degli alunni di scuole statali.

3 Legislative decree n. 297 of 1994 approved the unified text (Testo Unico) on education. The text has been amended and modified several times, but the principle expressed by Article 111 about the possibility of fulfilling the compulsory education requirement by way of parental education has been reaffirmed, in particular by various other decrees and ministerial circulars (the most recent, applying to school year 2014/2015 is Circular of the Ministry of Education n. 28 of 10 January 2014 http://www.istruzione.it/allegati/2014/cm28_14.pdf).

4 See Art. 114 of legislative decree n. 297 of 1994; Art. 2.1 of decree of the Ministry of Education n. 489 of 13 December 2001.

5 This is regulated by different ministerial documents, among others are the abovementioned ministerial decree n. 489 of 2001 (art. 2.7); note by the Ministry of Education n. 5693 of 20 June 2005.

È prescritto un esame di Stato per l'ammissione ai vari ordini e gradi di scuole o per la conclusione di essi e per l'abilitazione all'esercizio professionale.
Le istituzioni di alta cultura, università ed accademie, hanno il diritto di darsi ordinamenti autonomi nei limiti stabiliti dalle leggi dello Stato.

Art. 34.
La scuola è aperta a tutti.
L'istruzione inferiore, impartita per almeno otto anni, è obbligatoria e gratuita.
I capaci e meritevoli, anche se privi di mezzi, hanno diritto di raggiungere i gradi più alti degli studi.
La Repubblica rende effettivo questo diritto con borse di studio, assegni alle famiglie ed altre provvidenze, che devono essere attribuite per concorso.

Decreto Legislativo 16 aprile 1994, n. 297—*Testo Unico delle disposizioni legislative vigenti in materia di istruzione, relative alle scuole di ogni ordine e grado*[6]

Art. 111—Modalità di adempimento dell'obbligo scolastico
1. All'obbligo scolastico si adempie frequentando le scuole elementari e medie statali o le scuole non statali abilitate al rilascio di titoli di studio riconosciuti dallo Stato o anche privatamente, secondo le norme del presente testo unico.
2. I genitori dell'obbligato o chi ne fa le veci che intendano provvedere privatamente o direttamente all'istruzione dell'obbligato devono dimostrare di averne la capacità tecnica od economica e darne comunicazione anno per anno alla competente autorità.

7.2 Religious Education

In the past, the only religious education in state schools was the teaching of Catholicism: Article 36 of the Concordat of 1929 introduced compulsory religious (Catholic) education. The new agreement of 1984 between the state and the Catholic Church (Art. 9) revised this system: the teaching of Catholicism is voluntary and not compulsory, and it should not create discrimination, treat-

6 The text is available at http://www.normattiva.it/uri-res/N2Ls?urn:nir:stato:decreto.legislativo:1994-04-16;297 (in G.U. n. 115 of 19/5/1994, last accessed 2 February 2015).

ing unfavourably students who do not attend these lessons (this principle was stated by the Constitutional Court and reaffirmed in the already mentioned legislative decree n. 297 of 1994).[7]

The state assures the teaching of the Catholic religion in all non-university schools, while the teaching of other religions is possible under the conditions stipulated in the agreements with different denominations (for example, on the request of families, in accordance with the religious authorities and the management of the school, at no cost to the state). As Islam does not have an agreement with the state, the legislation of 1929–1930 still applies in this area. In particular, Article 23 of Royal decree n. 289/1930 states that religious denominations may use the classrooms of state schools for religious education, when there is a number of families requesting this and if there is no place of worship available with educational facilities. All the costs are paid by the denomination and an agreement between the religious group and the Director of the Regional School Office is necessary.

For the rest, Italian legislation does not contain any provision specifically devoted to religious education or to teaching *about* religion: religious education is seen as a matter concerning religious denominations and their relations with the state.[8]

One can mention some general provisions about the possibility of organising optional educational activities, free of charge and under the responsibility of the school, taking into account the interests and requests of families. This possibility is stated, for example, in Article 7 of decree n. 59 of 2004, defining the teaching programmes and objectives of the primary school cycle. The provision does not mention religious aspects, but lessons about religions may be included in such optional activities.

Regio decreto 28 febbraio 1930, n. 289—***Norme per l'attuazione della L. 24 giugno 1929, n. 1159, sui culti ammessi nello Stato e per il coordinamento di essa con le altre leggi dello Stato***

Art. 23
Quando il numero degli scolari lo giustifichi e quando per fondati motivi non possa esservi adibito il tempio, i padri di famiglia professanti un culto

7 See for example judgment n. 203/1989 of the Constitutional Court (at http://www.olir.it/documenti/?documento=370, last accessed 2 February 2015). Art. 311 of the legislative decree of 1997 is published below.

8 Cf. Ferrari, Alessandro, "La scuola italiana di fronte al paradigma Musulmano", in Ferrari, Alessandro (ed.), *Islam in Europa/Islam in Italia tra Diritto e Società*, cit., 171–198.

diverso dalla religione dello Stato possono ottenere che sia messo a loro disposizione qualche locale scolastico per l'insegnamento religioso dei loro figli: la domanda è diretta al provveditore agli studi il quale, udito il consiglio scolastico, può provvedere direttamente in senso favorevole. In caso diverso e sempre quando creda, ne riferisce al Ministero della Pubblica Istruzione, che decide di concerto con quello dell'Interno. Nel provvedimento di concessione dei locali si devono determinare i giorni e le ore nei quali l'insegnamento deve essere impartito e le opportune cautele.

Decreto Legislativo 16 aprile 1994, n. 297—*Testo Unico delle disposizioni legislative vigenti in materia di istruzione, relative alle scuole di ogni ordine e grado*
(s.o. G.U. n. 115 del 19/5/1994)

Art. 311—Diritti delle altre confessioni religiose diverse dalla cattolica
1. La Repubblica italiana, nel garantire la libertà di coscienza di tutti, riconosce agli alunni delle scuole pubbliche non universitarie, il diritto di avvalersi o di non avvalersi di insegnamenti religiosi.
2. Per dare reale efficacia all'attuazione del diritto di avvalersi o di non avvalersi di insegnamenti religiosi, si provvede a che l'insegnamento religioso ed ogni eventuale pratica religiosa, nelle classi in cui sono presenti alunni che hanno dichiarato di non avvalersene, non abbiano luogo in occasione dell'insegnamento di altre materie, né secondo orari che abbiano per i detti alunni effetti comunque discriminanti.
3. Per le confessioni religiose diverse dalla cattolica si osservano le disposizioni della legge 24 giugno 1929, n. 1159, in quanto applicabili, e quelle delle leggi emanate a seguito di intese tra lo Stato e singole confessioni religiose.
[…]

Decreto legislative 19 febbraio 2004, n. 59—*Definizione delle norme generali relative alla scuola dell'infanzia e al primo ciclo dell'istruzione, a norma dell'articolo 1 della legge 28 marzo 2003, n. 53*[9]

Art. 7—Attività educative e didattiche
1. Al fine di garantire l'esercizio del diritto-dovere di cui all'articolo 4, comma 1, l'orario annuale delle lezioni nella scuola primaria, comprensivo della quota

9 www.normattiva.it/uri-res/N2Ls?urn:nir:stato:decreto.legislativo:2004-02-19;59 (last access 2 February 2015).

riservata alle regioni, alle istituzioni scolastiche autonome e all'insegnamento della religione cattolica in conformità alle norme concordatarie di cui all'articolo 3, comma 1, ed alle conseguenti intese, è di 891 ore, oltre a quanto previsto al comma 2.
2. Le istituzioni scolastiche, al fine di realizzare la personalizzazione del piano di studi, organizzano, nell'ambito del piano dell'offerta formativa, tenendo conto delle prevalenti richieste delle famiglie, attività e insegnamenti, coerenti con il profilo educativo, per ulteriori 99 ore annue, la cui scelta è facoltativa e opzionale per gli allievi e la cui frequenza è gratuita. Gli allievi sono tenuti alla frequenza delle attività facoltative per le quali le rispettive famiglie hanno esercitato l'opzione. Le predette richieste sono formulate all'atto dell'iscrizione. Al fine di ampliare e razionalizzare la scelta delle famiglie, le istituzioni scolastiche possono, nella loro autonomia, organizzarsi anche in rete.
[...]
5. L'organizzazione delle attività educative e didattiche rientra nell'autonomia e nella responsabilità delle istituzioni scolastiche, fermo restando che il perseguimento delle finalità di cui all'articolo 5, assicurato dalla personalizzazione dei piani di studio, è affidato ai docenti responsabili delle attività educative e didattiche, previste dai medesimi piani di studio.
[...]
8. Le istituzioni scolastiche definiscono le modalità di svolgimento dell'orario delle attività didattiche sulla base del piano dell'offerta formativa, delle disponibilità strutturali e dei servizi funzionanti, fatta salva comunque la qualità dell'insegnamento-apprendimento.
9. Nell'organizzazione dell'orario settimanale i criteri della programmazione delle attività educative devono rispettare una equilibrata ripartizione dell'orario quotidiano tra le attività obbligatorie e quelle opzionali facoltative.

7.3 Private Schools

Article 33.3 of the Constitution entitles organisations and private individuals to set up schools and educational institutes at no cost to the state. Act n. 62 of 2000 has defined the rules on non-state schools. In particular, it establishes the requirements for recognising private schools on an equal basis with state schools, in accordance with Article 33.4 of the Constitution. Schools with equal status are called *scuole paritarie* and they are publicly subsidised;[10] they also

10 *Scuole paritarie* are indirectly financed through grants to pupils and tax relief for families;

have the authority to issue certificates with the same legal value as qualifications from state schools. Private schools are free to choose their own cultural orientation and educational-teaching approach (Art. 1.3, Act n. 62/2000). Legislation in force guarantees to students of private schools the same treatment as pupils who attend state schools (Art. 33.4 of the Constitution; Art. 1 of Act 62/2000).

According to law 62/2000 non-state schools are not obliged to apply for equality of status and schools with non-equal status (*scuole non paritarie*) can operate in Italy.[11]

As for religious schools, agreements signed between the state and religious denominations ensure the freedom to have and maintain denominational schools. For denominations without such an agreement (*intesa*), Article 24 of Royal decree n. 289 of 1930 gives recognised religious bodies the opportunity to open private schools at no cost to the state. Only bodies with legal personality can establish this type of school; the Italian Muslim community, of which the only recognised body is the Islamic Cultural Centre of Rome (see sect. 2.2.1), has never availed itself of this opportunity.

Among the non-state schools, one can also mention foreign schools, including schools of Muslim majority countries. Specific legislation deals with authorisations, opening, employment relations, and graduation titles of foreign schools.[12]

---

however, a direct form of financing is maintained for primary and pre-primary *scuole paritarie*. Direct financing has been in existence for a long time and it is maintained, considering that private and *paritarie* pre-primary schools are numerous and can cover a large part of the families' needs. Additional funds, provided by regional legislation, are sometimes established.

11 Act n. 27 of 3 February 2006 distinguishes between schools with equal status (*paritarie*) and merely private schools (*non paritarie*). The latter are free to act in Italy as long as their educational programmes do not conflict with Italian law; they are included in a specific list of the Regional School Office (see e.g. ministerial decree n. 82 of 10 October 2008); they cannot award graduation titles and pupils must pass exams if they wish to access the state education system (the same problem as with parental education: see sect. 7.1). To open a private school (*non paritaria*) individuals or organisations must comply with some requirements (qualification of teachers, safety of the buildings, etc.) and obtain authorisation from the local education authority.

12 See, in particular, Art. 366 of Legislative decree n. 297 of 1994, cit.; D.P.R. 18 April 1994, n. 389 'Regolamento recante semplificazione dei procedimenti di autorizzazione al funzionamento di scuole e di istituzioni culturali straniere in Italia'; decree of the Ministry of Education d.m. 13 Jan. 1999, n. 5 'Disciplina del funzionamento di scuole e istituzioni culturali straniere in Italia'; ministerial circular of the Ministry of Education of 25 January

Costituzione

Art. 33.
L'arte e la scienza sono libere e libero ne è l'insegnamento.
La Repubblica detta le norme generali sull'istruzione ed istituisce scuole statali per tutti gli ordini e gradi.
Enti e privati hanno il diritto di istituire scuole ed istituti di educazione, senza oneri per lo Stato.
La legge, nel fissare i diritti e gli obblighi delle scuole non statali che chiedono la parità, deve assicurare ad esse piena libertà e ai loro alunni un trattamento scolastico equipollente a quello degli alunni di scuole statali.
È prescritto un esame di Stato per l'ammissione ai vari ordini e gradi di scuole o per la conclusione di essi e per l'abilitazione all'esercizio professionale.
Le istituzioni di alta cultura, università ed accademie, hanno il diritto di darsi ordinamenti autonomi nei limiti stabiliti dalle leggi dello Stato.

Legge 10 marzo 2000 n. 62: ***Norme per la parità scolastica e disposizioni sul diritto allo studio e all'istruzione***[13]
(GU n. 67 del 21-3-2000)

Art. 1
1. Il sistema nazionale di istruzione, fermo restando quanto previsto dall'articolo 33, secondo comma, della Costituzione, è costituito dalle scuole statali e dalle scuole paritarie private e degli enti locali. La Repubblica individua come obiettivo prioritario l'espansione dell'offerta formativa e la conseguente generalizzazione della domanda di istruzione dall'infanzia lungo tutto l'arco della vita.
2. Si definiscono scuole paritarie, a tutti gli effetti degli ordinamenti vigenti, in particolare per quanto riguarda l'abilitazione a rilasciare titoli di studio aventi valore legale, le istituzioni scolastiche non statali, comprese quelle degli enti locali, che, a partire dalla scuola per l'infanzia, corrispondono agli ordinamenti generali dell'istruzione, sono coerenti con la domanda formativa

1999, n. 18 'Scuole ed organismi didattici e/o educativi stranieri in Italia. Delega di competenze'; Act 24 May 2002, n. 103 'Norme in materia di docenti di scuole e università straniere operanti in Italia'.

13 www.normattiva.it/uri-res/N2Ls?urn:nir:stato:legge:2000-03-10;62 (last accessed 2 February 2015).

delle famiglie e sono caratterizzate da requisiti di qualità ed efficacia di cui ai commi 4, 5 e 6.
3. Alle scuole paritarie private è assicurata piena libertà per quanto concerne l'orientamento culturale e l'indirizzo pedagogico-didattico. Tenuto conto del progetto educativo della scuola, l'insegnamento è improntato ai principi di libertà stabiliti dalla Costituzione. Le scuole paritarie, svolgendo un servizio pubblico, accolgono chiunque, accettandone il progetto educativo, richieda di iscriversi, compresi gli alunni e gli studenti con handicap. Il progetto educativo indica l'eventuale ispirazione di carattere culturale o religioso. Non sono comunque obbligatorie per gli alunni le attività extra-curriculari che presuppongono o esigono l'adesione ad una determinata ideologia o confessione religiosa.

Regio decreto 28 febbraio 1930, n. 289—*Norme per l'attuazione della L. 24 giugno 1929, n. 1159, sui culti ammessi nello Stato e per il coordinamento di essa con le altre leggi dello Stato*

Art. 24
Quando il numero degli alunni lo giustifichi, gli istituti eretti in ente morale, dei culti diversi dalla religione dello Stato possono essere autorizzati ad aprire, per i fedeli del rispettivo culto, scuole elementari da considerarsi, a termini delle disposizioni speciali vigenti, a sgravio totale o parziale degli obblighi delle amministrazioni scolastiche e dei comuni.
Ogni provvedimento in proposito spetta al Ministro della Pubblica Istruzione, che lo adotterà di concerto con quello dell'Interno.

CHAPTER 8

Further and Higher (Tertiary) Education

With regard to higher education, there is no specific provision in Italy concerning Islam. In fact, there is no legislation about the teaching of the Islamic religion in universities or other higher educational institutions and no rules on private universities with religious (including Islamic) character. Moreover, as has already been said, Italian schools do not provide Islamic education, in so far as Islam does not have an agreement with the state; in consequence, there is no regulation about the training of teachers of the Islamic religion.

With regard to imam training, a debate has very recently started. The consultative Committee on Islam (*Comitato per l'Islam*: see sect. 2) has published an advice on this issue,[1] summarising problems and possible solutions; among them is the development of a project about imam training organised by a partnership of universities.[2] In any case, despite this advice and the development of projects and debates on this issue, the Italian State has not yet approved any specific piece of legislation about imam training.

---

1 Comitato per l'Islam Italiano, *Parere su Imam e formazione* (Advice on Imam and training), 31 May 2011 http://www1.interno.gov.it/mininterno/export/sites/default/it/assets/files/21/0664_Comitato_per_Islam._parere_del_31_maggio_su_imam_e_formazione.pdf (last accessed 26 January 2015).

2 A course for religious leaders has been organised for three years. It was not a proper imam training course, but one about the legal and general characteristics of Italian society in order to develop integration and a better knowledge of different issues related to religion.

CHAPTER 9

Islamic Chaplaincy in Public Institutions

Rules on chaplaincy are often included in various pieces of legislation concerning the functioning of the public institutions concerned. Such rules reiterate the religious freedom of every person staying in a hospital, prison, centre for immigrants, or serving in the armed forces, and their right to receive spiritual care from a minister of their religion. For each of the institutions mentioned we can find a different set of rules.

With regard to the armed forces, legislative decree n. 66 of 2010 adopted a sort of "code" on the military system, including a provision (Art. 1471) on freedom of religion and the right of soldiers to receive religious assistance on request. Paragraph 5 of Article 1471 refers to the specific conditions on pastoral care established in the Concordat of 1984 and in the agreements with other denominations; these specific conditions are not determined for Islam, as there is no agreement with the state, so the general conditions established in the legislation of 1929–1930 apply.

In prisons, religious freedom is granted to all inmates. They can practise their religion and request spiritual care from a minister of their religion (Art. 26, par. 1 and 4, of Act n. 354 of 1974; Art. 58 of d.p.r. n. 230 of 2000), in accordance with principles of human dignity and non-discrimination (Art. 1 of Act n. 354/1975). Religion is considered an element of rehabilitation and re-integration into society (Arts. 1 and 15 of Act n. 354/1975). An authorisation is needed for ministers of religions without an agreement with the state (e.g. Islam) to access prisons and offer religious assistance (Art. 67 of Act n. 354/1975; Arts. 58 and 116 of d.p.r. n. 230/2000). Often, other provisions are used to that end: for example Article 17 of Act n. 354/1975 provides that every association or individual interested in cooperating for the rehabilitation of prisoners may ask for an authorisation to access and to offer assistance to the inmates. This is not a proper chaplaincy activity, but Muslim communities have considered this possibility, because it is often difficult to demonstrate the qualification as ministers of religion of imams or Muslim leaders in accordance with Italian legislation (verification of their qualification is necessary under Art. 116 of d.p.r. n. 230 of 2000).

With regard to chaplaincy in hospitals, Article 38 of Act n. 833 of 1978 (establishing the National Health Service, *Servizio sanitario nazionale*) recognises the freedom of religion, and it states that everyone has the right to receive pastoral care according to their freedom of conscience. The chaplaincy service shall be organised through specific agreements with the religious leaders operating in the area where the hospital is located. As some issues about the health service are now under the competences of Regions (according to legislative decree n. 299 of 1999 and amendments), the organisation of pastoral care and the conclusion of specific agreements have often been determined by the regional or local authorities. In a few cases (e.g. in Florence[1]) the city hospital signed an agreement with the local Muslim community to regulate the presence of Muslim ministers of religion as chaplains.

As we can see, in almost every provision about the issue, the organisation of spiritual assistance—and, in particular, the rules on access of ministers of religion—is to be regulated by subsequent specific rules. The Catholic Church and religious denominations with *intese* enjoy special treatment because they have established the functioning of chaplaincy in their agreement with the state; in particular, they have specified the ministers who are allowed as chaplains in the different public institutions. For Islam (as for other religions without *intesa*), the problem is to define the conditions of religious assistance and the persons who can be appointed as chaplains. Apart from the sporadic cases in which agreements have been signed (for example concerning hospitals, at the local level), one must refer to decree n. 289 of 1930. Articles 5, 6 and 8 give to all ministers of "admitted cults" the opportunity to access public institutions using an authorisation by the person responsible from the institution concerned. A similar provision is included in Act n. 354 of 1975 (Art. 67) and d.p.r. n. 230 of 2000 (Arts. 58 and 116) on prisons. Only for chaplaincy in the army, the abovementioned decree n. 289/1930 establishes that a minister of religion shall be appointed as chaplain only when he is approved by the state, in accordance with Article 3 of Act n. 1159 of 1929. In the other cases, the authorisation by the person responsible of the public institution is sufficient to give access to the buildings and pastoral care to people who requested it.

Italian legislation has established some rules about spiritual care also for those who are staying in centres for the reception of immigrants. Article 21 of d.p.r. n. 394 of 1999 grants religious freedom to immigrants and states that ministers of religion shall have the right to access the centres and give religious assistance. However, there is no specific provision on how this assistance shall be organised, or about the persons admitted to the centres.

1 Protocollo di intesa 26 gennaio 2005, n. 33, *Umanizzazione del percorso clinico. Approvazione del Protocollo d'intesa con la Comunità Islamica per l'assistenza religiosa di pazienti di* A.O.U.C. ("Humanization of clinical environment. Enactment of the protocol of agreement with the Islamic community for the religious assistance of the patients of the Careggi Hospital"). Text available at http://www.olir.it/documenti/index.php?argomento=0&documento=2226 (last accessed 26 January 2015).

Regio decreto n. 289/1930. ***Norme per l'attuazione della legge 24 giugno 1929, n. 1159/1929, sui culti ammessi nello Stato e per il coordinamento di essa con le altre leggi dello Stato***

Art. 5
I ministri dei culti ammessi nello stato possono essere autorizzati a frequentare i luoghi di cura e di ritiro per prestare l'assistenza religiosa ai ricoverati che la domandino.
L'autorizzazione è data da chi è preposto alla direzione amministrativa del luogo di cura o di ritiro e deve indicare le modalità o le cautele con cui l'assistenza deve essere prestata.

Art. 6
I ministri dei culti ammessi nello stato possono essere autorizzati a prestare l'assistenza religiosa agli internati negli istituti di prevenzione e di pena, ogni qualvolta ne siano richiesti dagli internati stessi o dai familiari o da chi abbia la tutela giuridica dei medesimi, sotto l'osservanza delle norme contenute nei regolamenti speciali per detti istituti.

Art. 8
In caso di mobilitazione delle forze armate dello Stato, l'assistenza religiosa dei militari acattolici, da esercitarsi da ministri di un culto ammesso nello Stato la nomina dei quali sia stata approvata a termini dell'art. 3 della legge, può essere autorizzata dall'autorità militare cui è stata affidata la suprema direzione delle operazioni belliche.
Alla stessa autorità spetta di stabilire le norme e le cautele con le quali tale assistenza può essere esercitata.

Decreto legislativo 15 marzo 2010, n. 66. ***Codice dell'ordinamento militare***[2]

Art. 1471—*Libertà di culto*
1. I militari possono esercitare il culto di qualsiasi religione e ricevere l'assistenza dei loro ministri.
2. La partecipazione alle funzioni religiose nei luoghi militari è facoltativa, salvo che nei casi di servizio.

2 www.normattiva.it/uri-res/N2Ls?urn:nir:stato:decreto.legislativo:2010-03-15;66 (last accessed 2 February 2015).

3. In ogni caso, compatibilmente con le esigenze di servizio il comandante del corpo o altra Autorità superiore rende possibile ai militari che vi hanno interesse la partecipazione ai riti della religione professata e a quelle iniziative rivolte ai militari, sia singolarmente sia collettivamente, che sono proposte e dirette dal personale addetto all'assistenza spirituale alle Forze armate.
4. Se un militare infermo, o per esso i suoi familiari, richiede i conforti della sua religione, i Ministri di questa sono chiamati ad assisterlo.
5. Rimane ferma la disciplina introdotta dalle leggi di autorizzazione alla ratifica ed esecuzione del Concordato lateranense, nonché dalle leggi che recepiscono le intese con le confessioni religiose diverse da quella cattolica.

Legge 23 dicembre 1978, n. 833. ***Istituzione del servizio sanitario nazionale***[3]
(*GU n. 360 del 28-12-1978—Suppl. Ordinario*)

Art. 38. *Servizio di assistenza religiosa*
Presso le strutture di ricovero del servizio sanitario nazionale è assicurata l'assistenza religiosa nel rispetto della volontà e della libertà di coscienza del cittadino.
A tale fine l'unità sanitaria locale provvede per l'ordinamento del servizio di assistenza religiosa cattolica d'intesa con gli ordinari diocesani competenti per territorio; per gli altri culti d'intesa con le rispettive autorità religiose competenti per territorio.

Legge 26 luglio 1975, n. 354. ***Norme sull'ordinamento penitenziario e sulla esecuzione delle misure privative e limitative della libertà***[4]
(GU n. 212 del 9-8-1975—Suppl. Ordinario)

Art. 1. *Trattamento e rieducazione*
Il trattamento penitenziario deve essere conforme ad umanità e deve assicurare il rispetto della dignità della persona.
Il trattamento è improntato ad assoluta imparzialità, senza discriminazioni in ordine a nazionalità, razza e condizioni economiche e sociali, a opinioni politiche e a credenze religiose.
[...]

3 www.normattiva.it/uri-res/N2Ls?urn:nir:stato:legge:1978-12-23;833 (last accessed 27 January 2015).

4 www.normattiva.it/uri-res/N2Ls?urn:nir:stato:legge:1975-07-26;354!vig=2015-01-27 (last accessed 27 January 2015).

Nei confronti dei condannati e degli internati deve essere attuato un trattamento rieducativo che tenda, anche attraverso i contatti con l'ambiente esterno, al reinserimento sociale degli stessi. Il trattamento è attuato secondo un criterio di individualizzazione in rapporto alle specifiche condizioni dei soggetti.

Art. 15. *Elementi del trattamento*
Il trattamento del condannato e dell'internato è svolto avvalendosi principalmente dell'istruzione, del lavoro, della religione, delle attività culturali, ricreative e sportive e agevolando opportuni contatti con il mondo esterno ed i rapporti con la famiglia.
[...]

Art. 17. *Partecipazione della comunità esterna all'azione rieducativa*
La finalità del reinserimento sociale dei condannati e degli internati deve essere perseguita anche sollecitando ed organizzando la partecipazione di privati e di istituzioni o associazioni pubbliche o private all'azione rieducativa.
Sono ammessi a frequentare gli istituti penitenziari con l'autorizzazione e secondo le direttive del magistrato di sorveglianza, su parere favorevole del direttore, tutti coloro che avendo concreto interesse per l'opera di risocializzazione dei detenuti dimostrino di potere utilmente promuovere lo sviluppo dei contatti tra la comunità carceraria e la società libera.
Le persone indicate nel comma precedente operano sotto il controllo del direttore.

Art. 26. *Religione e pratiche di culto*
I detenuti e gli internati hanno libertà di professare la propria fede religiosa, di istruirsi in essa e di praticarne il culto.
Negli istituti è assicurata la celebrazione dei riti del culto cattolico.
A ciascun istituto è addetto almeno un cappellano.
Gli appartenenti a religione diversa dalla cattolica hanno diritto di ricevere, su loro richiesta, l'assistenza dei ministri del proprio culto e di celebrarne i riti.

Art. 67. *Visite agli istituti*
Gli istituti penitenziari possono essere visitati senza autorizzazione da:
e) l'ordinario diocesano per l'esercizio del suo ministero;
[...]
Possono accedere agli istituti, con l'autorizzazione del direttore, i ministri del culto cattolico e di altri culti.

Decreto del Presidente della Repubblica 30 giugno 2000, n. 230. ***Regolamento recante norme sull'ordinamento penitenziario e sulle misure privative e limitative della libertà***[5]
(GU n. 195 del 22-8-2000—Suppl. Ordinario n. 131)

Art. 58. *Manifestazioni della libertà religiosa*
1. I detenuti e gli internati hanno diritto di partecipare ai riti della loro confessione religiosa purché compatibili con l'ordine e la sicurezza dell'istituto e non contrari alla legge, secondo le disposizioni del presente articolo.
2. È consentito ai detenuti e agli internati che lo desiderino di esporre, nella propria camera individuale o nel proprio spazio di appartenenza nella camera a più posti, immagini e simboli della propria confessione religiosa.
3. È consentito, durante il tempo libero, a singoli detenuti e internati di praticare il culto della propria professione religiosa, purché non si esprima in comportamenti molesti per la comunità.
4. Per la celebrazione dei riti del culto cattolico, ogni istituto è dotato di una o più cappelle in relazione alle esigenze del servizio religioso. Fino all'entrata in vigore delle disposizioni di esecuzione dell'intesa di cui all'articolo 11, comma 2, dell'accordo, con protocollo addizionale, firmato a Roma il 18 febbraio 1984, che apporta modificazioni al Concordato lateranense dell'11 febbraio 1929, tra la Repubblica italiana e la Santa Sede, ratificato e reso esecutivo con la legge 25 marzo 1985, n. 121, le pratiche di culto, l'istruzione e l'assistenza spirituale dei cattolici sono assicurate da uno o più cappellani in relazione alle esigenze medesime; negli istituti in cui operano più cappellani, l'incarico di coordinare il servizio religioso è affidato ad uno di essi dal provveditore regionale dell'amministrazione penitenziaria, ovvero, se trattasi di istituti per minorenni, dal direttore del centro per la giustizia minorile, sentito l'ispettore dei cappellani.
5. Per l'istruzione religiosa o le pratiche di culto di appartenenti ad altre confessioni religiose, anche in assenza di ministri di culto, la direzione dell'istituto mette a disposizione idonei locali.
6. La direzione dell'istituto, al fine di assicurare ai detenuti e agli internati che ne facciano richiesta, l'istruzione e l'assistenza spirituale, nonché la celebrazione dei riti delle confessioni diverse da quella cattolica, si avvale dei ministri di culto indicati da quelle confessioni religiose i cui rapporti con lo Stato italiano sono regolati con legge; si avvale altresì dei ministri di culto indicati a

5 www.normattiva.it/uri-res/N2Ls?urn:nir:stato:decreto.del.presidente.della.repubblica:2000-06-30;230!vig=2015-01-27 (last accessed 27 January 2015).

tal fine dal Ministero dell'interno; può, comunque, fare ricorso, anche fuori dei casi suindicati, a quanto disposto dall'articolo 17, secondo comma, della legge[6].

Art. 116. *Accesso di ministri di culto agli istituti*
1. I ministri del culto cattolico, diversi dai cappellani, e quelli indicati nell'ultimo comma dell'articolo 58 sono autorizzati dal direttore, su richiesta di singoli detenuti o internati, ad accedere all'istituto, per attività del loro ministero, previo accertamento della loro qualità. Tale attività si svolge in modo da assicurare la necessaria riservatezza.

Decreto del Presidente della Repubblica 31 agosto 1999, n. 394. ***Regolamento recante norme di attuazione del testo unico delle disposizioni concernenti la disciplina dell'immigrazione e norme sulla condizione dello straniero, a norma dell'articolo 1, comma 6, del decreto legislativo 25 luglio 1998, n. 286***[7]
(GU n. 258 del 3-11-1999—Suppl. Ordinario n. 190)

Art. 21. *Modalità del trattenimento*
1. Le modalità del trattenimento devono garantire, nel rispetto del regolare svolgimento della vita in comune, la libertà di colloquio all'interno del centro e con visitatori provenienti dall'esterno, in particolare con il difensore che assiste lo straniero, e con i ministri di culto, la libertà di corrispondenza, anche telefonica, ed i diritti fondamentali della persona fermo restando l'assoluto divieto per lo straniero di allontanarsi dal centro.
2. Nell'ambito del centro sono assicurati, oltre ai servizi occorrenti per il mantenimento e l'assistenza degli stranieri trattenuti o ospitati, i servizi sanitari essenziali, gli interventi di socializzazione e la libertà del culto nei limiti previsti dalla Costituzione.
[...]
7. Oltre al personale addetto alla gestione dei centri e agli appartenenti alla forza pubblica, al giudice competente e all'autorità di pubblica sicurezza, ai centri possono accedere i familiari conviventi e il difensore delle persone trattenute o ospitate, i ministri di culto, il personale della rappresentanza diplomatica o consolare, e gli appartenenti ad enti, associazioni del volontariato e

6 It refers to Art. 17 of Act n. 354 of 1975 (d.P.R. n. 230 of 2000 is the regulation implementing the Act of 1975).

7 www.normattiva.it/uri-res/N2Ls?urn:nir:presidenza.repubblica:decreto.del.presidente.della.repubblica:1999-08-31;394 (last accessed 26 January 2015).

cooperative di solidarietà sociale, ammessi a svolgervi attività di assistenza a norma dell'articolo 22 ovvero sulla base di appositi progetti di collaborazione concordati con il prefetto della provincia in cui è istituito il centro.

CHAPTER 10

Employment and Social Law

10.1 Employment Law

Italian legislation on employment relations considers religious aspects with regard to different issues: first, the rights of employees (including freedom of religion) and non-discrimination; secondly the status of religious denominations and bodies as employers.

This latter issue is not regulated by specific Acts, except for Article 4 of Act n. 108 of 1990, which excludes protection against discriminatory dismissal where the employer is pursuing a non-profit-making activity of a religious or ideological nature. In other words, religious employers can discriminate on the ground of religion; this is confirmed by legislative decree n. 216 of 2003 (Art. 3.5), transposing Directive n. 2000/78 of the EU on discrimination in employment.

As for the protection of the religious freedom rights of employees, we can mention Article 15 of the so-called 'Statute of workers' (Act n. 300/1970) prohibiting religious discrimination; Article 4 of Act n. 604 of 1966 prohibiting discriminatory dismissal; Articles 43 and 44 of legislative decree n. 286 of 1998 on immigration, which reiterate the prohibition of religious and racial discrimination in employment and in other areas. The already mentioned legislative decree n. 216 of 2003 has established new definitions of direct and indirect discrimination, the prohibition of harassment (also on grounds of religion) and procedural guarantees against discrimination, according to the EU legislation on this issue. A general protection of religious freedom is also enshrined in Articles 1 and 8 of the Statute of workers, which set out the freedom of expression and the protection of personal data within employment relations.

Legge 20 maggio 1970, n. 300. ***Norme sulla tutela della libertà e dignità dei lavoratori, della libertà sindacale e dell'attività sindacale nei luoghi di lavoro e norme sul collocamento***[1]
(Gazz. Uff. 27 maggio 1970, n. 131)

1 www.normattiva.it/uri-res/N2Ls?urn:nir:stato:legge:1970-05-20;300!vig=2015-01-29 (last accessed 29 January 2015).

Art. 1. *Libertà di opinione*
I lavoratori, senza distinzione di opinioni politiche, sindacali e di fede religiosa, hanno diritto, nei luoghi dove prestano la loro opera, di manifestare liberamente il proprio pensiero, nel rispetto dei principi della Costituzione e delle norme della presente legge.

Art. 8. *Divieto di indagini sulle opinioni.*
È fatto divieto al datore di lavoro, ai fini dell'assunzione, come nel corso dello svolgimento del rapporto di lavoro, di effettuare indagini, anche a mezzo di terzi, sulle opinioni politiche, religiose o sindacali del lavoratore, nonché su fatti non rilevanti ai fini della valutazione dell'attitudine professionale del lavoratore.

Art. 15. *Atti discriminatori*
È nullo qualsiasi patto od atto diretto a:
a) subordinare l'occupazione di un lavoratore alla condizione che aderisca o non aderisca ad una associazione sindacale ovvero cessi di farne parte;
b) licenziare un lavoratore, discriminarlo nella assegnazione di qualifiche o mansioni, nei trasferimenti, nei provvedimenti disciplinari, o recargli altrimenti pregiudizio a causa della sua affiliazione o attività sindacale ovvero della sua partecipazione ad uno sciopero.
Le disposizioni di cui al comma precedente si applicano altresì ai patti o atti diretti a fini di discriminazione politica, religiosa, razziale, di lingua o di sesso, di handicap, di età o basata sull'orientamento sessuale o sulle convinzioni personali.

Legge 11 maggio 1990, n. 108. *Disciplina dei licenziamenti individuali*[2]
(GU n. 108 del 11-5-1990)

Art. 3. *Licenziamento discriminatorio*
1. Il licenziamento determinato da ragioni discriminatorie ai sensi dell'articolo 4 della legge 15 luglio 1966, n. 604, e dell'articolo 15 della legge 20 maggio 1970, n. 300, come modificato dall'articolo 13 della legge 9 dicembre 1977, n. 903, è nullo indipendentemente dalla motivazione addotta e comporta, quale che sia il numero dei dipendenti occupati dal datore di lavoro, le conseguenze previste dall'articolo 18 della legge 20 maggio 1970, n. 300, come modificato dalla presente legge. Tali disposizioni si applicano anche ai dirigenti.

2 www.normattiva.it/uri-res/N2Ls?urn:nir:stato:legge:1990-05-11;108 (last accessed 27 January 2015).

Art. 4. *Area di non applicazione*
1. Fermo restando quanto previsto dall'articolo 3, le disposizioni degli articoli 1 e 2 non trovano applicazione nei rapporti disciplinati dalla legge 2 aprile 1958, n. 339. La disciplina di cui all'articolo 18 della legge 20 maggio 1970, n. 300, come modificato dall'articolo 1 della presente legge, non trova applicazione nei confronti dei datori di lavoro non imprenditori che svolgono senza fini di lucro attività di natura politica, sindacale, culturale, di istruzione ovvero di religione o di culto.
[...]

Decreto legislativo 25 luglio 1998, n. 286. ***Testo unico delle disposizioni concernenti la disciplina dell'immigrazione e norme sulla condizione dello straniero***[3]
(Gazz. Uff. 18 agosto 1998, n. 191, s.o.)

Art. 43. *Discriminazione per motivi razziali, etnici, nazionali o religiosi.*
1. Ai fini del presente capo, costituisce discriminazione ogni comportamento che, direttamente o indirettamente, comporti una distinzione, esclusione, restrizione o preferenza basata sulla razza, il colore, l'ascendenza o l'origine nazionale o etnica, le convinzioni e le pratiche religiose, e che abbia lo scopo o l'effetto di distruggere o di compromettere il riconoscimento, il godimento o l'esercizio, in condizioni di parità, dei diritti umani e delle libertà fondamentali in campo politico, economico, sociale e culturale e in ogni altro settore della vita pubblica.
2. In ogni caso compie un atto di discriminazione:
a) il pubblico ufficiale o la persona incaricata di pubblico servizio o la persona esercente un servizio di pubblica necessità che nell'esercizio delle sue funzioni compia od ometta atti nei riguardi di un cittadino straniero che, soltanto a causa della sua condizione di straniero o di appartenente ad una determinata razza, religione, etnia o nazionalità, lo discriminino ingiustamente;
b) chiunque imponga condizioni più svantaggiose o si rifiuti di fornire beni o servizi offerti al pubblico ad uno straniero soltanto a causa della sua condizione di straniero o di appartenente ad una determinata razza, religione, etnia o nazionalità;

3 www.normattiva.it/uri-res/N2Ls?urn:nir:stato:decreto.legislativo:1998-07-25;286 (last accessed 27 January 2015).

c) chiunque illegittimamente imponga condizioni più svantaggiose o si rifiuti di fornire l'accesso all'occupazione, all'alloggio, all'istruzione, alla formazione e ai servizi sociali e socio-assistenziali allo straniero regolarmente soggiornante in Italia soltanto in ragione della sua condizione di straniero o di appartenente ad una determinata razza, religione, etnia o nazionalità;
d) chiunque impedisca, mediante azioni od omissioni, l'esercizio di un'attività economica legittimamente intrapresa da uno straniero regolarmente soggiornante in Italia, soltanto in ragione della sua condizione di straniero o di appartenente ad una determinata razza, confessione religiosa, etnia o nazionalità;
e) il datore di lavoro o i suoi preposti i quali, ai sensi dell'articolo 15 della legge 20 maggio 1970, n. 300, come modificata e integrata dalla legge 9 dicembre 1977, n. 903, e dalla legge 11 maggio 1990, n. 108, compiano qualsiasi atto o comportamento che produca un effetto pregiudizievole discriminando, anche indirettamente, i lavoratori in ragione della loro appartenenza ad una razza, ad un gruppo etnico o linguistico, ad una confessione religiosa, ad una cittadinanza. Costituisce discriminazione indiretta ogni trattamento pregiudizievole conseguente all'adozione di criteri che svantaggino in modo proporzionalmente maggiore i lavoratori appartenenti ad una determinata razza, ad un determinato gruppo etnico o linguistico, ad una determinata confessione religiosa o ad una cittadinanza e riguardino requisiti non essenziali allo svolgimento dell'attività lavorativa.
3. Il presente articolo e l'articolo 44 si applicano anche agli atti xenofobi, razzisti o discriminatori compiuti nei confronti dei cittadini italiani, di apolidi e di cittadini di altri Stati membri dell'Unione europea presenti in Italia[4].

Art. 44. *Azione civile contro la discriminazione.*
1. Quando il comportamento di un privato o della pubblica amministrazione produce una discriminazione per motivi razziali, etnici, nazionali o religiosi, il giudice può, su istanza di parte, ordinare la cessazione del comportamento pregiudizievole e adottare ogni altro provvedimento idoneo, secondo le circostanze, a rimuovere gli effetti della discriminazione.
[...]

4 The decree of 1998 is dedicated to the regulation of immigration and the rights of immigrants, but par. 3 of Art. 43 makes applicable also to Italian citizens the protection against discrimination and the procedural guarantees established in the following Art. 44.

Decreto legislativo 9 luglio 2003, n. 216. ***Attuazione della direttiva 2000/78/ CE per la parità di trattamento in materia di occupazione e di condizioni di lavoro.***[5]
(Gazzetta Ufficiale della Repubblica Italiana, n. 187 del 13 agosto 2003)

Art. 1. *Oggetto*
1. Il presente decreto reca le disposizioni relative all'attuazione della parità di trattamento fra le persone indipendentemente dalla religione, dalle convinzioni personali, dagli handicap, dall'età e dall'orientamento sessuale, per quanto concerne l'occupazione e le condizioni di lavoro, disponendo le misure necessarie affinché tali fattori non siano causa di discriminazione, in un'ottica che tenga conto anche del diverso impatto che le stesse forme di discriminazione possono avere su donne e uomini.

Art. 2. *Nozione di discriminazione*
1. Ai fini del presente decreto e salvo quanto disposto dall'articolo 3, commi da 3 a 6, per principio di parità di trattamento si intende l'assenza di qualsiasi discriminazione diretta o indiretta a causa della religione, delle convinzioni personali, degli handicap, dell'età o dell'orientamento sessuale. Tale principio comporta che non sia praticata alcuna discriminazione diretta o indiretta, così come di seguito definite:
a) discriminazione diretta quando, per religione, per convinzioni personali, per handicap, per età o per orientamento sessuale, una persona è trattata meno favorevolmente di quanto sia, sia stata o sarebbe trattata un'altra in una situazione analoga;
b) discriminazione indiretta quando una disposizione, un criterio, una prassi, un atto, un patto o un comportamento apparentemente neutri possono mettere le persone che professano una determinata religione o ideologia di altra natura, le persone portatrici di handicap, le persone di una particolare età o di un orientamento sessuale in una situazione di particolare svantaggio rispetto ad altre persone.
2. È fatto salvo il disposto dell'articolo 43, commi 1 e 2 del testo unico delle disposizioni concernenti la disciplina dell'immigrazione e norme sulla condizione dello straniero, approvato con decreto legislativo 25 luglio 1998, n. 286.
3. Sono, altresì, considerate come discriminazioni, ai sensi del comma 1, anche le molestie ovvero quei comportamenti indesiderati, posti in essere per uno

5 www.normattiva.it/uri-res/N2Ls?urn:nir:stato:decreto.legislativo:2003-07-09;216 (last accessed 27 January 2015).

dei motivi di cui all'articolo 1, aventi lo scopo o l'effetto di violare la dignità di una persona e di creare un clima intimidatorio, ostile, degradante, umiliante od offensivo.
4. L'ordine di discriminare persone a causa della religione, delle convinzioni personali, dell'handicap, dell'età o dell'orientamento sessuale è considerata una discriminazione ai sensi del comma 1.

Art. 3. *Ambito di applicazione*
1. Il principio di parità di trattamento senza distinzione di religione, di convinzioni personali, di handicap, di età e di orientamento sessuale si applica a tutte le persone sia nel settore pubblico che privato ed è suscettibile di tutela giurisdizionale secondo le forme previste dall'articolo 4, con specifico riferimento alle seguenti aree:
a) accesso all'occupazione e al lavoro, sia autonomo che dipendente, compresi i criteri di selezione e le condizioni di assunzione;
b) occupazione e condizioni di lavoro, compresi gli avanzamenti di carriera, la retribuzione e le condizioni del licenziamento;
c) accesso a tutti i tipi e livelli di orientamento e formazione professionale, perfezionamento e riqualificazione professionale, inclusi i tirocini professionali;
d) affiliazione e attività nell'ambito di organizzazioni di lavoratori, di datori di lavoro o di altre organizzazioni professionali e prestazioni erogate dalle medesime organizzazioni.
2. La disciplina di cui al presente decreto fa salve tutte le disposizioni vigenti in materia di:
a) condizioni di ingresso, soggiorno ed accesso all'occupazione, all'assistenza e alla previdenza dei cittadini dei Paesi terzi e degli apolidi nel territorio dello Stato;
b) sicurezza e protezione sociale;
c) sicurezza pubblica, tutela dell'ordine pubblico, prevenzione dei reati e tutela della salute;
d) stato civile e prestazioni che ne derivano;
e) forze armate, limitatamente ai fattori di età e di handicap.
3. Nel rispetto dei principi di proporzionalità e ragionevolezza, nell'ambito del rapporto di lavoro o dell'esercizio dell'attività di impresa, non costituiscono atti di discriminazione ai sensi dell'articolo 2 quelle differenze di trattamento dovute a caratteristiche connesse alla religione, alle convinzioni personali, all'handicap, all'età o all'orientamento sessuale di una persona, qualora, per la natura dell'attività lavorativa o per il contesto in cui essa viene espletata, si tratti di caratteristiche che costituiscono un requisito essenziale e determi-

nante ai fini dello svolgimento dell'attività medesima. Parimenti, non costituisce atto di discriminazione la valutazione delle caratteristiche suddette ove esse assumano rilevanza ai fini dell'idoneità allo svolgimento delle funzioni che le forze armate e i servizi di polizia, penitenziari o di soccorso possono essere chiamati ad esercitare.

4. Sono, comunque, fatte salve le disposizioni che prevedono accertamenti di idoneità al lavoro per quanto riguarda la necessità di una idoneità ad uno specifico lavoro e le disposizioni che prevedono la possibilità di trattamenti differenziati in merito agli adolescenti, ai giovani, ai lavoratori anziani e ai lavoratori con persone a carico, dettati dalla particolare natura del rapporto e dalle legittime finalità di politica del lavoro, di mercato del lavoro e di formazione professionale.

5. Non costituiscono atti di discriminazione ai sensi dell'articolo 2 le differenze di trattamento basate sulla professione di una determinata religione o di determinate convinzioni personali che siano praticate nell'ambito di enti religiosi o altre organizzazioni pubbliche o private, qualora tale religione o tali convinzioni personali, per la natura delle attività professionali svolte da detti enti o organizzazioni o per il contesto in cui esse sono espletate, costituiscano requisito essenziale, legittimo e giustificato ai fini dello svolgimento delle medesime attività.

6. Non costituiscono, comunque, atti di discriminazione ai sensi dell'articolo 2 quelle differenze di trattamento che, pur risultando indirettamente discriminatorie, siano giustificate oggettivamente da finalità legittime perseguite attraverso mezzi appropriati e necessari. In particolare, resta ferma la legittimità di atti diretti all'esclusione dallo svolgimento di attività lavorativa che riguardi la cura, l'assistenza, l'istruzione e l'educazione di soggetti minorenni nei confronti di coloro che siano stati condannati in via definitiva per reati che concernono la libertà sessuale dei minori e la pornografia minorile.

Art. 4. *Tutela giurisdizionale dei diritti*

[...]

2. La tutela giurisdizionale avverso gli atti e i comportamenti di cui all'articolo 2 si svolge nelle forme previste dall'articolo 44, commi da 1 a 6, 8 e 11, del testo unico delle disposizioni concernenti la disciplina dell'immigrazione e norme sulla condizione dello straniero, approvato con decreto legislativo 25 luglio 1998, n. 286.

3. Chi intende agire in giudizio per il riconoscimento della sussistenza di una delle discriminazioni di cui all'articolo 2 e non ritiene di avvalersi delle procedure di conciliazione previste dai contratti collettivi, può promuovere

il tentativo di conciliazione ai sensi dell'articolo 410 del codice di procedura civile o, nell'ipotesi di rapporti di lavoro con le amministrazioni pubbliche, ai sensi dell'articolo 66 del decreto legislativo 30 marzo 2001, n. 165, anche tramite le rappresentanze locali di cui all'articolo 5.
4. Il ricorrente, al fine di dimostrare la sussistenza di un comportamento discriminatorio a proprio danno, può dedurre in giudizio, anche sulla base di dati statistici, elementi di fatto, in termini gravi, precisi e concordanti, che il giudice valuta ai sensi dell'articolo 2729, primo comma, del codice civile.
5. Con il provvedimento che accoglie il ricorso il giudice, oltre a provvedere, se richiesto, al risarcimento del danno anche non patrimoniale, ordina la cessazione del comportamento, della condotta o dell'atto discriminatorio, ove ancora sussistente, nonché la rimozione degli effetti. Al fine di impedirne la ripetizione, il giudice può ordinare, entro il termine fissato nel provvedimento, un piano di rimozione delle discriminazioni accertate.
6. Il giudice tiene conto, ai fini della liquidazione del danno di cui al comma 5, che l'atto o comportamento discriminatorio costituiscono ritorsione ad una precedente azione giudiziale ovvero ingiusta reazione ad una precedente attività del soggetto leso volta ad ottenere il rispetto del principio della parità di trattamento.
7. Il giudice può ordinare la pubblicazione del provvedimento di cui ai commi 5 e 6, a spese del convenuto, per una sola volta su un quotidiano di tiratura nazionale.
8. Resta salva la giurisdizione del giudice amministrativo per il personale di cui all'articolo 3, comma 1, del decreto legislativo 30 marzo 2001, n. 165.

Art. 5. *Legittimazione ad agire*
1. Le rappresentanze locali delle organizzazioni sindacali maggiormente rappresentative a livello nazionale, in forza di delega, rilasciata per atto pubblico o scrittura privata autenticata, a pena di nullità, sono legittimate ad agire ai sensi dell'articolo 4, in nome e per conto o a sostegno del soggetto passivo della discriminazione, contro la persona fisica o giuridica cui è riferibile il comportamento o l'atto discriminatorio.
2. Le rappresentanze locali di cui al comma 1 sono, altresì, legittimate ad agire nei casi di discriminazione collettiva qualora non siano individuabili in modo diretto e immediato le persone lese dalla discriminazione.

10.1.1 *Religious Needs in Employment and Provisions on Days of Rest*

With regard to specific claims about the religious needs of workers, Italian legislation is not so specific. For example, there are no specific provisions on the use of religious clothes at work, nor about accommodations for dietary needs in workplace canteens.

One of the issues concerning religious freedom at work considered by the Italian legislation is the regulation of holidays and days of rest. Provisions on this issue can be found in some Acts about employment relations which provide for the right to have a weekly day of rest, normally Sunday;[6] Sunday work is permitted if it is justified by the nature of the work (e.g. public transport). These provisions are justified by traditions rather than religious motives.

With regard to holidays, a number of Christian holidays have been incorporated into the official calendar of recognised days of rest (for example Assumption day on 15 August and Christmas). In the agreements with some religious denominations (Jewish, Adventist Church), it is established that an employer shall assure the weekly day of rest on Saturday, instead of Sunday, and a free day during the religious holidays established by the *intese*. This right is granted if the organisation and the needs of the workplace are not compromised and according to the flexibility of the job.

Islam and other denominations without an agreement with the state can benefit from such rights only if the employer establishes appropriate measures in the specific contracts. This was the case of workers in the province of Ragusa, who were given special permits for Islamic holidays, in particular during the month of Ramadan (provincial contract, in force in 2000–2003);[7] and of diplomatic officials belonging to the Islamic or Jewish religion, who can benefit from a different weekly day of rest (collective contract adopted with decree of the President of the Republic n. 107 of 2006). Moreover, Act n. 339 of 1958 on domestic work states that employers shall assure time off to domestic staff in order to permit them to respect their civic duties and religious needs.

6 See for example Art. 36 of the Constitution and Art. 2109 of the civil code on the right of workers to have a weekly day of rest; Act n. 370 of 22 February 1934 (at http://www.normattiva.it/uri-res/N2Ls?urn:nir:stato:legge:1934-02-22;370, last accessed 27 January 2015); Art. 9 of legislative decree n. 66 of 2003 (at http://www.normattiva.it/uri-res/N2Ls?urn:nir:stato:decreto.legislativo:2003-04-08;66, last accessed 27 January 2015).

7 Available at http://www.olir.it/documenti/?documento=4357 (last accessed 29 January 2015).

Legge 2 aprile 1958, n. 339 ***Per la tutela del rapporto di lavoro domestico***
(GU n. 93 del 17-4-1958)[8]

Art. 6. *Diritti e doveri*
Il lavoratore è tenuto a:
prestare la propria opera con la dovuta diligenza secondo le necessità e gli interessi della famiglia per la quale lavora, seguendo le disposizioni dei datori di lavoro;
Il datore di lavoro è tenuto a:
[...]
lasciare al lavoratore il tempo necessario per adempiere agli obblighi civili ed ai doveri essenziali del suo culto.

Decreto Presidente della Repubblica 20 gennaio 2006, n. 107. ***Recepimento dell'accordo sindacale per il quadriennio giuridico 2004–2007 e per il biennio economico 2004–2005, riguardante il personale della carriera diplomatica, relativamente al servizio prestato in Italia, ai sensi dell'articolo 112 del decreto del Presidente della Repubblica 5 gennaio 1967, n. 18, come sostituito dall'articolo 14 del decreto legislativo 24 marzo 2000, n. 85.***
(da "Gazzetta Ufficiale della Repubblica Italiana" n. 66 del 20 marzo 2006)[9]

Art. 4. *Congedo ordinario, giornate di riposo e festività.*
[...]
12. Sono considerati festivi le domeniche e gli altri giorni riconosciuti come tali dalla legge a tutti gli effetti civili.
[...]
14. I funzionari diplomatici appartenenti alle religioni ebraica ed islamica, nonchè alle altre confessioni religiose riconosciute dallo Stato, hanno il diritto di fruire, a richiesta, di un giorno di riposo settimanale diverso da quello

8 www.normattiva.it/uri-res/N2Ls?urn:nir:stato:legge:1958-04-02;339 (last accessed 29 January 2015). The text published here is that in force, with amendments introduced by legislative decree n. 196 of 30 June 2003 on the protection of personal data ("Codice in materia di protezione dei dati personali").

9 Available at www.normattiva.it/uri-res/N2Ls?urn:nir:stato:decreto.del.presidente.della.repubblica:2006-01-20;107 (last accessed 29 January 2015). The collective contract was approved for the years 2004–2007 but the provision on days of rest is still in force, since it was not repealed by the subsequent contracts.

domenicale. In questo caso il tempo di lavoro non prestato dal funzionario diplomatico viene recuperato in altri giorni lavorativi, d'intesa con il responsabile della struttura.

10.2 Social Law

With regard to social law, we can mention the provisions on the social security system. Act n. 903 of 1973 established a pension scheme for all ministers of religion who receive payment for their functions. In the agreements between religious denominations and the state (*intese*) there are specific rules on employment relations of ministers within the religious bodies; in any case, all ministers, including those of denominations without *intesa*, can apply for the pension scheme established in Act n. 903/1973, on certain conditions. In particular, ministers must be resident in Italy or be Italian citizens and, according to the Act, their religious community shall conclude a dedicated agreement with the Ministry of the Interior. This specific agreement can be concluded even if the religious denomination is not recognised under the legislation of 1929–1930; for the moment no such agreement has been signed with any Muslim group. Documents regarding the appointment as minister of religion are necessary in order to apply for the pension scheme, which is run by the National Pensions Agency (INPS).[10]

Another issue related to religion and the social security system is polygamous marriages. In a message, the National Pensions Agency has specified that with regard to family allowances only one marriage shall be taken into account in the case of polygamous unions (see sect. 15.2).[11]

10 See http://www.inps.it/portale/default.aspx?lastMenu=5924&iMenu=1 (last accessed 27 January 2015).

11 INPS (National Pension Agency): message of 29 September 2006, n. 25928, 'Assegno per il nucleo familiare in caso di poligamia' (on family maintenance policy in case of polygamy, available at http://www.olir.it/documenti/?documento=3927, last accessed 27 January 2015).

Legge 22 dicembre 1973, n. 903, ***Istituzione del Fondo di previdenza del clero e dei ministri di culto delle confessioni religiose diverse dalla cattolica e nuova disciplina dei relativi trattamenti pensionistici***[12]
(GU n. 9 del 10-1-1974)

Art. 1. *Unificazione dei fondi del clero e dei ministri di culto delle confessioni religiose diverse dalla cattolica: istituzione di un Fondo unico.*
È istituito presso l'Istituto nazionale della previdenza sociale il "Fondo di previdenza per il clero secolare e per i ministri di culto delle confessioni religiose diverse dalla cattolica" che nel presente e negli articoli seguenti è indicato con la parola "Fondo".
[...]

Art. 5. *Soggetti all'obbligo dell'iscrizione al Fondo*
Sono soggetti all'obbligo dell'iscrizione al Fondo tutti i sacerdoti secolari, nonché tutti i ministri di culto delle confessioni religiose diverse dalla cattolica aventi cittadinanza italiana, residenti in Italia[13], dal momento della loro ordinazione sacerdotale o dall'inizio del ministero di culto in Italia fino alla data di decorrenza della pensione di vecchiaia ovvero della pensione di invalidità. Con decreto del Ministro per l'interno, previe intese con le rappresentanze delle singole confessioni religiose diverse dalla cattolica che ne facciano richiesta, si provvede all'applicazione della presente legge con le modalità del caso.
Per l'accertamento delle condizioni di cui al primo comma, riguardanti l'attività di culto, è richiesta:
[...]
2) per i ministri di culto delle confessioni religiose diverse dalla cattolica, l'attestazione da parte dei competenti organi della rispettiva confessione.
[...]

12 www.normattiva.it/uri-res/N2Ls?urn:nir:stato:legge:1973-12-22;903 (last accessed 27 January 2015).

13 Art. 42.6 of Act n. 488 of 1999 has extended the pension scheme to ministers of religion who are resident in Italy, even if they are not Italian citizens: "Art. 42.6: A decorrere dal 1 gennaio 2000 l'iscrizione al Fondo di cui al comma 1 è estesa ai sacerdoti e ai ministri di culto non aventi cittadinanza italiana e presenti in Italia al servizio di diocesi italiane e delle Chiese o enti acattolici riconosciuti, nonché ai sacerdoti e ai ministri di culto aventi cittadinanza italiana, operanti all'estero al servizio di diocesi italiane e delle Chiese o enti acattolici riconosciuti."

CHAPTER 11

Islamic Slaughter and Food Regulation

Religious slaughter was made lawful in Italy in 1928, when a Royal decree about general measures on slaughter, authorised religious slaughtering methods, provided that the death of the animals was caused as fast as possible.[1] Islamic and Jewish traditions exclude the stunning of animals—normally performed before killing, in order to avoid animals' suffering—and provide that slaughter must be carried out through a cut. Italian legislation in force authorises slaughter without prior stunning, according to the Jewish and Islamic rules, by a ministerial decree of 1980. This possibility was confirmed by Legislative Decree n. 333 of 1 September 1998, transposing EU Directive n. 93/119 "on the protection of animals at the time of slaughter or killing". These provisions specify the conditions under which such practice is to be performed: the person who carries out the killing of the animal has to be qualified; the slaughtering process has to respect sanitary rules, etc. Further details on methods of slaughtering are included in EU Regulation n. 1099/2009 of 24 September 2009 on the protection of animals at the time of killing.[2]

It is worth noting that the decree of 1980 refers to the role of religious communities in performing ritual slaughter, mentioning the Jewish Communities Union in Italy and the Islamic Cultural Centre, which is the only recognised Islamic body. As a matter of fact, ritual slaughter is carried out not just by this centre. The decree of 1980 also mentions the purpose for permitting Islamic slaughter, namely the export of meat to Muslim majority countries; today the situation has changed and this method is part of the religious freedom of the Italian Muslim community.

Religious freedom also concerns the ability to respect Islamic dietary rules in public institutions (e.g. schools, prisons and hospitals) or at work. In this regard, there is no specific provision at the national level, except for a reference in decree (d.P.R.) n. 230 of 2000 on the penitentiary system: Article 11 states that meals shall be prepared taking into account, as far as possible, different religious dietary requirements. The consideration of religious needs shall be "as

1 Royal Decree n. 3298 of 20 December 1928 concerning the rules for the sanitary supervision of meats.

2 Not published here, see http://eur-lex.europa.eu/legal-content/EN/ALL/?uri=CELEX:32009R1099 (last accessed 10 April 2015).

far as possible", so the implementation of the right to have a *halal* meal often depends on the organisation of the specific institution in question.

Different religious dietary needs are normally taken into account in the organisation of school canteens and in the preparation of meals in hospitals, but there is no legal obligation in this sense. Thus, the accommodation of dietary needs is done in a pragmatic way, sometimes through (formal or informal) agreements (for example, the already mentioned provincial contract of workers of Ragusa, which recognised the need to respect Ramadan;[3] and some regulations of the municipal authorities on the organisation of school canteens[4]).

Decreto Ministeriale 11 giugno 1980. ***Autorizzazione alla macellazione degli animali secondo i riti religiosi ebraico e islamico***
(Gazzetta Ufficiale della Repubblica italiana, n. 168 del 20 giugno 1980)

Il Ministero della Sanità di concerto con il Ministero dell'Interno

[...]
Accertato che la Unione delle Comunità israelitiche italiane con nota n. 21 novembre 1979 prot. N. 1834/50 indirizzata al Ministero dell'Interno ha richiesto che ai sensi della legge n. 439 sia data autorizzazione alle Comunità israelitiche italiane di procedere alla macellazione degli animali secondo le modalità del rito ebraico;
Accertato che il Centro islamico culturale d'Italia con nota prot. 340/79.AA del 30 novembre 1979 ha richiesto che sia data autorizzazione alle Comunità islamiche italiane di procedere alla macellazione degli animali secondo le modalità del rito islamico;
Visto che le Comunità israelitiche e il Centro islamico sono stati riconosciuti enti morali, la prima con regi decreti 30 ottobre 1930. n. 1731 e 24 settembre 1931, n. 1279, il secondo con il decreto del Presidente della Repubblica 21 dicembre 1974, n. 712;
Atteso altresì che da parte di paesi di religione islamica che non dispongono di sufficienti strutture ed impianti per la macellazione esistono richieste

3 See sect. 10.1.1.

4 See the regulation reproduced below of the municipality of Fiorenzuola d'Arda: it simply states that the menus will take into account the religious needs of children. Other examples are published in Chizzoniti, Antonio G. (ed.), *Religione e autonomie locali. La tutela della libertà religiosa nei territori di Cremona, Lodi e Piacenza*, Tricase (Le): Libellula Edizioni, 2014.

di importazione dall'Italia di carni bovine, ovine ed equine macellate nel territorio nazionale;
Considerato che detti paesi pongono come condizione inderogabile per importare le carni di cui sopra che la macellazione avvenga nel rispetto del rito islamico;
[...]

Decreta:

Art. 1
Si autorizza la macellazione senza preventivo stordimento eseguita secondo i riti ebraico ed islamico da parte delle rispettive comunità.

Art. 2
La macellazione deve essere effettuata da personale qualificato che sia perfettamente a conoscenza ed addestrato nell'esecuzione dei rispettivi metodi rituali.
L'operazione dovrà essere effettuata mediante un coltello affilatissimo in modo che possano essere recisi con un unico taglio contemporaneamente l'esofago, la trachea ed i grossi vasi sanguigni del collo.

Art. 3
Nel corso della operazione debbono essere adottate tutte le precauzioni atte ad evitare il più possibile sofferenze ed ogni stato di eccitazione non necessario. A tal fine gli animali debbono essere introdotti nella sala di macellazione solo quando tutti i preparativi siano stati completati. Il contenimento, la preparazione e la iugulazione dei medesimi debbono essere eseguiti senza alcun indugio.

Art. 4
Può essere autorizzata la macellazione senza preventivo stordimento eseguita secondo il rito islamico nei macelli riconosciuti idonei all'esportazione di carni ai sensi dell'art. 7 del decreto del Presidente della Repubblica 11 febbraio 1961 n. 264 a condizione che:
1) la macellazione avvenga nel rispetto delle disposizioni di cui ai precedenti articoli 2 e 3;
2) i titolari di detti macelli ne facciano espressa richiesta, ai fini dell'esportazione nei Paesi islamici al Ministero della sanità, che, previo sopralluogo, procederà ad accertare che esistano le condizioni a che gli animali vengano macellati in conformità delle disposizioni di cui agli articoli n. 2 e 3.

Decreto legislativo 1 settembre 1998, n. 333. ***Attuazione della direttiva 93/119/CE relativa alla protezione degli animali durante la macellazione o l'abbattimento***
(Da "Gazzetta Ufficiale della Repubblica Italiana" n. 226 del 28 settembre 1998)

Art. 2
Ai fini del presente decreto si intende per:
a) macello: qualsiasi stabilimento o attrezzatura, comprese le attrezzature per il trasferimento e la stabulazione degli animali, utilizzati per la macellazione a fini commerciali degli animali di cui all'articolo 5, comma 1;
b) trasferimento: lo scarico di animali o il loro trasporto dalle piattaforme di scarico, dai recinti o dalle stalle dei macelli, fino ai locali o ai luoghi di macellazione;
c) stabulazione: la custodia di animali in stalle, recinti o spazi coperti, nonché aree aperte utilizzati nei macelli, allo scopo di prestare loro, eventualmente, le cure necessarie (acqua, foraggio, riposo) prima della macellazione;
d) immobilizzazione: qualsiasi sistema inteso a limitare i movimenti degli animali per facilitare uno stordimento o abbattimento efficaci;
e) stordimento: qualsiasi procedimento che, praticato sugli animali, determina rapidamente uno stato di incoscienza che si protrae fino a quando non intervenga la morte;
f) abbattimento: qualsiasi procedimento che produca la morte dell'animale;
g) macellazione: l'uccisione dell'animale mediante dissanguamento;
h) autorità competente: Il Ministero della sanità, il servizio veterinario della regione o provincia autonoma, il veterinario ufficiale quale definito dall'art. 2, comma 1, lettera g), del decreto legislativo 18 aprile 1994, n. 286, e successive modifiche; tuttavia per le macellazioni secondo determinati riti religiosi, l'autorità competente in materia di applicazione e controllo delle disposizioni particolari relative alla macellazione secondo i rispettivi riti religiosi è l'autorità religiosa per conto della quale sono effettuate le macellazioni; questa opera sotto la responsabilità del veterinario ufficiale per le altre disposizioni contenute nel decreto.
2. I titolari di stabilimenti di macellazione presso i quali si intende macellare secondo determinati riti religiosi comunicano all'autorità sanitaria veterinaria territorialmente competente, per il successivo inoltro al Ministero della sanità, di essere in possesso dei requisiti prescritti.

Art. 5
I solipedi, i ruminanti, i suini, i conigli e i volatili da cortile, trasportati nei macelli ai fini della macellazione, devono essere:

[...]
c) storditi prima della macellazione o abbattuti istantaneamente conformemente alle indicazioni di cui all'allegato C.
2. Le disposizioni di cui al comma 1, lettera c), non si applicano alle macellazioni che avvengono secondo i riti religiosi di cui all'art. 2, comma 1, lettera h).

Decreto del Presidente della Repubblica 30 giugno 2000, n. 230. ***Regolamento recante norme sull'ordinamento penitenziario e sulle misure privative e limitative della libertà.***[5]

Art. 11. *Vitto giornaliero*
1. Ai detenuti e agli internati vengono somministrati giornalmente tre pasti.
2. Il regolamento interno stabilisce l'orario dei pasti in modo tale che il primo possa essere consumato non lontano dalla sveglia, il secondo dopo circa cinque ore dal primo ed il terzo dopo circa sei ore dal secondo.
3. Ai minorenni vengono somministrati giornalmente quattro pasti opportunamente intervallati.
4. Le tabelle vittuarie, distinte in riferimento ai criteri di cui al primo comma dell'articolo 9 della legge, sono approvate con decreto ministeriale ai sensi del comma quarto dello stesso articolo, in conformità del parere dell'Istituto superiore della nutrizione.
Le tabelle vittuarie devono essere aggiornate almeno ogni cinque anni. Nella formulazione delle tabelle vittuarie si deve anche tenere conto, in quanto possibile, delle prescrizioni proprie delle diverse fedi religiose.

Comune di Fiorenzuola d'Arda (Provincia di Piacenza). ***Regolamento per il servizio di mensa scolastica,*** **28 aprile 2008, n. 16**[6]

Art. 8—Tabelle dietetiche e diete speciali
Le tabelle dietetiche vengono predisposte dall'Azienda Sanitaria Locale sulla base del computo calorico ottimale per ciascuna categoria di bambini; il menù è articolato su 6 settimane. Inoltre allo scopo di garantire pasti più variati ed appetibili è differenziato per stagione (un menù invernale e uno primaverile).

5 Cit. in ch. 9.
6 Available at http://www.olir.it/documenti/?documento=6277 (last accessed 29 January 2015).

Le tabelle suddette sono disponibili presso l'Ufficio Pubblica Istruzione per tutti coloro che volessero prenderne visione.
Il menù della mensa scolastica è proposto a livello generale e non può essere variato sulla base di preferenze individuali.
Sono previste diete speciali solo per bambini che abbiano particolari problemi di salute (allergie alimentari, morbo celiaco, ecc.); la somministrazione di dieta particolare dovrà essere richiesta allegando certificato medico rinnovato annualmente. Il menù può essere modificato, su specifica richiesta, per esigenze di tipo religioso.
[...]

CHAPTER 12

Islamic Goods and Services

Italian legislation on goods and services normally does not take into account Islamic needs. An exception to the lack of specific regulations in this area is an inter-ministerial agreement promoting the *halal* certification issued by one of the main Muslim organizations in Italy, the Co.Re.Is.

The Co.Re.Is. has applied to the Italian Patents and Trademarks Office for the registration of its *halal* quality mark, called "Halal Italia",[1] and a pilot project was launched by the Milan Chamber of Commerce in order to promote the certification. The label "Halal Italia" is intended to certify the conformity to Islamic law of food products, cosmetics, pharmaceuticals and also services, e.g. travel companies. In 2010 the competent ministries (Foreign Affairs, Economy, Health and Agriculture) signed an inter-ministerial convention with the aim of promoting this registered brand and fostering the commerce of this kind of products and services, especially in the international trade with Muslim majority countries. As we noticed about rules on ritual slaughter, the importance of economic reasons is specifically underlined in the agreement, rather than the role of similar certifications for the religious needs of Muslims in Italy.

It is worth noting that "Halal Italia" is described as a voluntary certification system: it does not certify all *halal* products in Italy and there is no obligation to use a religious certification. Enterprises and firms can obtain a licence to use the *halal* quality stamp if they comply with the set of rules published by the Co.Re.Is. organisation; national and international rules on health and security of foods and products must also be respected.

Convenzione interministeriale di sostegno all'iniziativa "Halal Italia" tra il Ministero degli Affari Esteri, il Ministero dello Sviluppo Economico, il Ministero della Salute, il Ministero delle Politiche Agricole, Alimentari e Forestali, 30 giugno 2010[2]

1 See the website at http://www.halalitalia.org/ (last accessed on 29 January 2015).

2 Available at http://www.halalitalia.org/documenti/Conv.%20Interm.firmata.pdf; English version at http://www.halalitalia.org/documenti/Interministerial%20Agreement_Halal%20Italia.pdf (both accessed 29 January 2015).

Il Ministero degli Affari Esteri, il Ministero dello Sviluppo Economico, il Ministero della Salute, il Ministero delle Politiche Agricole, Alimentari e Forestali
– convinti dell'esigenza di sostenere l'internazionalizzazione del sistema produttivo italiano, la tutela del made in Italy e la promozione degli interessi italiani all'estero;
– alla luce della crescente domanda da parte degli operatori economici italiani di strumenti innovativi per l'internazionalizzazione;
– tenuto conto del crescente interesse manifestato dagli operatori economici italiani per i mercati del mondo islamico;
– prendendo atto dell'avvenuta presentazione presso l'Ufficio italiano Brevetti e Marchi da parte della Co.Re.Is. Italiana della richiesta di registrazione di un marchio di qualità "halal" (consentito), valido per tutto il territorio nazionale, che certifichi la conformità alle leggi coraniche di prodotti alimentari, cosmetici e farmaceutici prodotti in Italia;
– alla luce della positiva esperienza del "Progetto-pilota Halal" della Camera di Commercio di Milano, finalizzato alla guida e all'accreditamento dei produttori lombardi nel mercato islamico nazionale e internazionale, promosso dall'Azienda speciale per le Attività Internazionali della Camera di Commercio di Milano, PROMOS, in partnership con Co.Re.Is. Italiana

Si impegnano a:
Promuovere presso le Associazioni di categoria e le imprese potenzialmente interessate il suddetto marchio e le opportunità che esso offre in termini di penetrazione dei mercati dei Paesi a maggioranza islamica;
Accreditare presso le Autorità dei Paesi islamici il marchio registrato da parte della Co.Re.Is. Italiana come certificazione di qualità riconosciuta dallo Stato italiano per l'esportazione di prodotti conformi alle leggi coraniche.

A tal fine:
– Fermo restando l'obbligo per le aziende italiane aderenti al suddetto marchio di rispettare le prescrizioni della normativa italiana in materia di produzione ed immissione sul mercato;
– Fatte salve le disposizioni vigenti in materia di sicurezza sanitaria degli alimenti, nonché quelle in materia di sicurezza dei cosmetici e dei prodotti farmaceutici;
– fatta salva l'esigenza per le aziende aderenti all'iniziativa, in quanto operanti in Italia, di rispettare regole e procedure stabilite dall'Unione europea riguardo alla produzione, al trattamento e alla commercializzazione dei prodotti

Il Ministero degli Affari esteri e il Ministero dello Sviluppo Economico si impegnano ad organizzare, in collaborazione con Co.Re.Is. Italiana, la Camera di Commercio di Milano/PROMOS e il sistema camerale italiano, eventi promozionali di presentazione del marchio di qualità "halal" sopra descritto, sulla base anche delle indicazioni del Ministero della Salute e del Ministero delle Politiche Agricole, Alimentari e Forestali, ai quali verranno invitate a partecipare le principali Associazioni di categoria potenzialmente coinvolte e le aziende italiane interessate ad accedere ai mercati del mondo islamico.

Ampia diffusione all'iniziativa verrà data sulle pagine web del Ministero degli Affari Esteri, del Ministero dello Sviluppo Economico, del Ministero della Salute, del Ministero delle Politiche Agricole, Alimentari e Forestali, nonché presso le Rappresentanze Diplomatiche e Consolari italiane e gli Uffici ICE in Italia e all'estero.
Il Ministero dello Sviluppo Economico provvederà ad organizzare, in collaborazione con la Co.Re.Is. Italiana, la Camera di Commercio di Milano/PROMOS, il sistema camerale italiano, le Associazioni di categoria e gli Enti locali eventualmente interessati, specifici corsi di formazione in favore degli imprenditori che intenderanno aderire alla suddetta iniziativa di certificazione.

In raccordo con il Ministero dello Sviluppo Economico, il Ministero della Salute e il Ministero delle Politiche Agricole, Alimentari e Forestali, il Ministero degli Affari Esteri provvederà a rendere noto in maniera adeguata alle Autorità dei Paesi a religione islamica l'avvenuta creazione del marchio di qualità garantendo—previa verifica da parte dei competenti organismi nazionali che le regole di produzione rispettino la normativa italiana e comunitaria in materia di sicurezza alimentare, di protezione del consumatore e di benessere animale—che i prodotti italiani dotati della suddetta certificazione sono conformi alle leggi coraniche.
Le Rappresentanze Diplomatiche e Consolari italiane e gli Uffici ICE all'estero svolgeranno un'adeguata azione promozionale presso le Autorità, le Associazioni imprenditoriali e le aziende dei Paesi islamici potenzialmente interessate all'iniziativa. Adeguata assistenza verrà garantita dalle Rappresentanze Diplomatiche e Consolari italiane e dagli Uffici ICE all'estero a tutte le aziende italiane aderenti all'iniziativa nelle attività volte a presentare i propri prodotti nei Paesi islamici.

Nel pieno rispetto della normativa comunitaria in materia di concorrenza e aiuti di Stato, specifiche iniziative promozionali, in Italia e all'estero, potranno essere a tal fine organizzate in coordinamento tra il Ministero degli Affari

Esteri, il Ministero dello Sviluppo Economico, il Ministero della Salute e il Ministero delle Politiche Agricole, Alimentari e Forestali.

Fatto a Roma, il 30 giugno 2010.

CHAPTER 13

Islamic Dress

In Italy there are no specific restrictions on dress, including that with a religious meaning. The wearing of headscarves is not prohibited in public places, at school, at work, or in similar circumstances. Religious attire is allowed also when photos for identity cards are taken, provided that the face is visible and recognisable, as stated in circulars of the Ministry of the Interior n. 4/1995 and 14/07/2000.[1] There have been a very few cases on this issue, mostly about the wearing of a full veil (burqa or niqab) and not about the headscarf.

A prohibition is established by Article 5 of Act n. 152 of 1975 on articles of dress that cover the face. The Act was approved during the period of internal political terrorism and it refers generally to all garments that can hinder the recognition of a person, banning them during public demonstrations for public security reason. This prohibition is not directed either intentionally or explicitly at religious dress; recently some proposed bills were intended to insert an express reference to the burqa in the 1975 Act, but they never became law.[2]

On the basis of the public security legislation, as amended in 2008, power has been given to local authorities to legislate on specific and urgent matters relating to urban safety and public security.[3] In consequence, some mayors

1 Circular of the Ministry of the Interior n. 4 of 14 March 1995, 'Rilascio carta di identità a cittadini professanti culti religiosi diversi da quello cattolico—uso del copricapo' (available at http://www.olir.it/documenti/?documento=1588, last accessed 2 February 2015); Circular of the Ministry of the Interior, Dipartimento della Pubblica Sicurezza, n. 300 of 24 July 2000 (available at http://www.olir.it/documenti/?documento=1530, last accessed 2 February 2015). The circulars refer to Art. 289 of Royal Decree n. 635 of 1940 that prohibits identity card photos with hats: on this point, they specify that the Islamic veil or similar religious attire is not a simple headgear but it is something characterising the person and must be shown in the passport photo.

2 For example bill n. 2422 proposed in 2009 (http://nuovo.camera.it/126?tab=1&leg=16&idDocumento=2422&sede=&tipo=, last accessed 2 February 2015). Draft laws on the prohibition of the burqa consider this garment both a violation of women's dignity and a danger for national security. On this issue see Ferrari, Alessandro, 'A Besieged Right: Religious Freedom and the Italian War on the Burqa and the Niqab', in Ferrari, A. and Pastorelli, S. (eds.), *The Burqa Affair Across Europe*, Farnham: Ashgate, 2013, pp. 37–58.

3 Mayors can enact provisions on matters of public security, in accordance with Art. 54.4 of legislative decree n. 267 of 18 August 2000, as amended by Art. 6 of decree law n. 92 of 2008

have enacted ordinances against the burqa/niqab. In the ordinance of Azzano Decimo of 2009 it is interesting to note that clothes like the burqa are thought to be the cause of suspicion and anxiety in the population and an obstacle to the development of civic society; the ban, justified also for security reasons, is applied only in certain public situations (sport, public markets, etc.).

Case Law

The Council of State decided the annulment of the ordinance of the mayor of Azzano Decimo (Pordenone) banning the *burqa* and the *niqab*.[4] The protection of public order and public security does not justify a blanket ban on full veils, because it is always possible to ask the person to identify herself, removing the veil, when necessary. The burqa, which is considered a cultural tradition and an expression of religious freedom, can be prohibited in some particular cases and circumstances when there is a specific necessity (for example to recognise people in a particular public space (decision 19 June 2008, n. 3076[5])).

In the same vein, the National Council of Judges (Consiglio Superiore della Magistratura) declared in a resolution that once a person has been identified, he/she can appear in judicial hearings with the face covered (resolution 22 February 2012[6]). This resolution followed a case in which a Muslim man wearing a turban was obliged to remove the garment in order to attend the court hearing. The tribunal had not considered discriminatory the rule prohibiting all headgear in court, without taking into account religious needs (ordinance of the investigation judge of the tribunal of Milan, 26 February 2009[7]).

(converted into Act n. 125 of 24 July 2008). The Constitutional Court has reduced the power of mayors, who can now adopt only urgent rules (judgment n. 115 of 7 April 2011). The text of Art. 54 is available at www.normattiva.it/uri-res/N2Ls?urn:nir:stato:decreto.legislativo:2000-08-18;267!vig=2015-02-04 (last accessed 4 February 2015).

4 The Council of State annulled ordinance n. 24 of 27 July 2004 of the mayor of Azzano Decimo. A following ordinance was approved in 2009 (reproduced here).

5 Available at http://www.olir.it/documenti/?documento=4721 (last accessed 2 February 2015).

6 Available at http://www.olir.it/documenti/index.php?argomento=127&documento=5782 (last accessed 2 February 2015).

7 http://www.olir.it/documenti/?documento=4938 (last accessed 2 February 2015).

Legge 22 maggio 1975, n. 152: ***Disposizioni a tutela dell'ordine pubblico.***
(da "Gazzetta Ufficiale della Repubblica Italiana" n. 136 del 24 maggio 1975)[8]

Art. 5
1. È vietato l'uso di caschi protettivi, o di qualunque altro mezzo atto a rendere difficoltoso il riconoscimento della persona, in luogo pubblico o aperto al pubblico, senza giustificato motivo. È in ogni caso vietato l'uso predetto in occasione di manifestazioni che si svolgano in luogo pubblico o aperto al pubblico, tranne quelle di carattere sportivo che tale uso comportino.
2. Il contravventore è punito con l'arresto da uno a due anni e con l'ammenda da 1.000 a 2.000 euro.

Comune di Azzano Decimo, ***Ordinanza in materia di uso di mezzi atti a rendere difficoltoso il riconoscimento della persona,*** **n. 03/2009 del 5 febbraio 2009**[9]

VISTO l'art. 54 del d.l.vo 18/08/2000, n. 267, così come modificato dall'art. 6 della L. nr. 125/08;
[…]
VISTO l'art. 5 della L. n. 152/75;
VISTO l'art. 26 della Carta dei valori, della cittadinanza e dell'integrazione, approvata con decreto del Ministero dell'Interno il 23/04/2007
[…]

APPRESA E RISCONTRATA: la sempre più evidente recrudescenza di episodi di criminalità e di degrado sociale atti a turbare l'ordine e la sicurezza pubblica anche comportanti l'uso di mezzi di qualsiasi genere atti a rendere difficoltoso il riconoscimento della persona (quali ad esempio caschi protettivi o capi di vestiario che in qualunque modo occultino parte del volto) specie in occasione di pubbliche manifestazioni o in concomitanza con esse;
che da tempo capita spesso di incontrare persone che usano, anche per tradizioni di costumi appartenenti ad altre etnie, indumenti particolari che comunque impediscono o rendono difficoltoso il riconoscimento di una persona in luogo pubblico o aperto al pubblico;

8 The text in force, as amended by Act n. 533 of 8 August 1977 and Act, n. 155 of 31 July 2005, is available at http://www.olir.it/documenti/?documento=2969 (last accessed 2 February 2015).
9 Available at http://www.olir.it/documenti/?documento=5157 (last accessed 2 February 2015).

che tali situazioni non possono trovare giuridicamente giustificato motivo che deroghi agli obblighi imposti dall'art. 5 della L. n. 152/1975, così come già richiamato dalla Autorità Nazionale di Pubblica Sicurezza nei decreti ministeriali di cui in premessa

AITESO che tali situazioni non sono sostenute da giustificati motivi e anzi:
– generano in alcuni casi nei cittadini un senso di paura, che ostacola il senso di identità e di appartenenza alla propria comunità nei canoni storicamente consolidati, con la conseguenza e il rischio che la popolazione tende a ritirarsi nella propria dimensione individuale e domestica, cosicché viene frenata la fruizione libera ed indisturbata degli spazi della città;
– tale paura danneggia il senso della felicità e quindi la qualità della vita e la qualità della convivenza urbana, svilendo i fini insiti nel contratto sociale che lega l'individuo ai gruppi e allo stato;

REPUTATO di voler aderire alla recente giurisprudenza in materia del Consiglio di Stato (decisione n. 3076/2008) con la quale il citato organo di rilievo costituzionale ha evidenziato come, in relazione al cosiddetto velo indossato per motivi religiosi "... le esigenze di pubblica sicurezza sono soddisfatte dal divieto di utilizzo in occasione di manifestazioni e dall'obbligo per tali persone di sottoporsi ad identificazione e alla rimozione del velo ove necessario a tal fine. Resta fermo che tale interpretazione non esclude che in determinati luoghi o da parte di specifici ordinamenti possano essere previste, anche in via amministrativa, regole comportamentali diverse incompatibili con il suddetto utilizzo, purché ovviamente trovino una ragionevole e legittima giustificazione sulla base di specifiche e settoriali esigenze ...",
di voler altresì rendere effettivo il dettato del citato art. 26 del D.M. Interno del 23/04/2007 il quale recita: "Non sono accettabili forme di vestiario che coprono il volto perché ciò impedisce il riconoscimento della persona e la ostacola nell'entrare in rapporto con gli altri".
[...]

DATO ATTO:
- che il presente provvedimento ha l'intento di garantire l'incolumità pubblica e l'integrità fisica della popolazione;
- che è volto al mantenimento della sicurezza urbana, intesa come bene pubblico da tutelare attraverso attività poste a difesa, nell'ambito delle comunità locali, del rispetto delle norme che regolano la vita civile, per migliorare le condizioni di vivibilità nei centri urbani, la convivenza civile e la coesione sociale;

- sulla scorta delle recenti novità normative il sindaco può esercitare il potere suddetto anche in modo discrezionale e finalizzato, nonché ha acquisito competenze in materia di sicurezza Pubblica;
- il presente provvedimento ha lo scopo di individuare le situazioni tipiche di questa comunità in cui possa verificarsi il pericolo per la sicurezza e l'incolumità delle persone
- il presente provvedimento è basato sulla base di specifiche e settoriali esigenze;

ORDINA

Che nelle giornate occasione di ogni tipo di manifestazione che si svolga in luogo pubblico o aperto al pubblico venga scrupolosamente rispettato, su tutto il territorio comunale, il disposto dell'art. 5. della L. 22.05.1975, n. 152, e particolarmente in occasione di:

- mercato settimanale del capoluogo;
- mercato settimanale della frazione di Tiezzo;
- partite di calcio delle squadre di Azzano Decimo, Tiezzo, Corva e Fagnigola;
- manifestazioni sportive in genere;
- la fiera della musica;
- i tradizionali festeggiamenti comunemente chiamati "sagre";
- tutte le manifestazioni per le quali vi è il patrocinio dell'amministrazione comunale;
- tutte le manifestazioni legittimamente autorizzate dall'amministrazione comunale e\o dall'autorità di pubblica sicurezza.

La Polizia Municipale è incaricata di vigilare sul rispetto della presente ordinanza

[...]

Comune di Drezzo (Como), Ordinanza del sindaco, n. 15 del 12 ottobre 2009. *Ordinanza in materia di tutela della sicurezza urbana e dell'incolumità pubblica.*[10]

PREMESSO CHE

Possono verificarsi in luoghi vari fenomeni di assembramento di persone, spesso legato al consumo di alcolici, tali da determinare turbamento e disturbo alla quiete pubblica;

10 Available at http://www.olir.it/documenti/?documento=5153 (last accessed 2 February 2015).

Nei luoghi pubblici e aperti al pubblico del territorio di Drezzo è possibile che si trattengano stranieri in violazione delle disposizioni di cui all'art. 1, comma 16 della legge 15 luglio 2009, n. 94;

[...]

Nei luoghi pubblici e aperti al pubblico è inoltre possibile che circolino persone con il volto coperto o con qualsivoglia copricapo (o velo) tale da renderne difficoltoso il riconoscimento

VISTO

Il decreto legge 23 maggio 2008, n. 92 recante "Misure urgenti in materia di sicurezza pubblica", convertito, con modificazioni, nella legge 24 luglio 2008, n. 125;

L'art. 54 del decreto legislativo 18 agosto 2000, n. 267, "Testo unico delle leggi sull'ordinamento degli enti locali" e successive modifiche ed integrazioni;

Il decreto del Ministero dell'Interno del 23 aprile 2007 relativo alla Carta dei valori della cittadinanza e dell'integrazione

[...]

ORDINA

[...]

5. È vietato l'utilizzo, se non per motivi di sicurezza, in tutti i luoghi pubblici e aperti al pubblico di qualsivoglia copricapo (o velo) che copra il viso e tale da rendere difficoltoso il riconoscimento della persona.

CHAPTER 14

Criminal Law

In Italian criminal law there are various provisions concerning religion. A first group includes Articles of the Criminal Code and legislation protecting against religious discrimination and religious hatred. These rules are of general character and can affect all religions.

The Criminal Code, after the last reform of 2006, penalises offences against religious denominations through the vilification of their members or ministers (Art. 403), by means of vilification or damage to objects of worship (Art. 404), and the disturbance of religious functions and acts of worship (Art. 405). Article 724 of the Code fines blasphemy against religions and offences made in public, against a deceased. These provisions of the Criminal Code were first introduced in 1930 in order to punish primarily offences against the Catholic religion, which at the time was the state religion. Since the adoption of the Constitution, decisions of the Constitutional Court have repealed the parts of the Code contradicting the principle of equality of all religions;[1] later, the reform of 2006 rewrote these Articles of the Criminal Code, trying also to establish a balance between the freedom of religion and the freedom of expression.

Other provisions that protect religions against offensive manifestation and hatred are included in Act n. 654 of 13 October 1975, as amended by Acts n. 205/1993 and n. 85/2006. Act n. 654 of 1975 was adopted to ratify the UN International Convention on the Elimination of All Forms of Racial Discrimination (ICERD); in Article 3 it includes a few provisions penalising the propagation of racial ideas, incitement to discriminate and acts of discrimination on grounds of race and religion (Art. 3.1.a); incitement to violence and hatred on grounds of race and religion (Art. 3.1.b); the setting up of associations and organisations with the purpose of promoting such ideas and acts (Art. 3.3).

---

1 See, among others, judgment of the Constitutional Court n. 329 of 1990 (available at http://www.olir.it/documenti/?documento=468, last accessed 29 January 2015): the Court affirmed that the protection of religious feelings is a corollary of the right to freedom of religion, which must be ensured to everyone, irrespective of the different contents of the religious communities.

Cases on Islamic hatred have been decided, applying these provisions. For example, in 2006, the Court of Cassation defined as a racist act a situation where a man insulted a Muslim woman and tried to take off her veil.[2]

A second category of rules concerns specific issues that are sometimes related to the Islamic religion. An example is the criminal offence of female genital mutilation. This is not a proper Muslim practice, but it concerns mainly immigrants, including those with a Muslim background. There are specific criminal law provisions on this issue: Act n. 7 of 2006 inserted into the criminal code two new Articles (Arts. 583 bis and 583 ter) prohibiting the performance of all forms of female genital mutilation. The terms of imprisonment are increased if the victim is a minor; health officers who practise or help in the commitment of genital mutilation shall also be debarred from the profession. The punishment applies also to foreigners residing in Italy who commit the offence while abroad.

With regard to male circumcision, this is not prohibited but there have been cases of circumcision not performed in hospitals but by private individuals, with resulting serious injuries, and a criminal conviction has followed (e.g. criminal tribunal of Milan, judgment of 26 November 1999[3]).

Finally, we can mention cases of culturally motivated crimes. Generally speaking, the criminal code establishes that the exercise of a right can justify an exception in the application of the criminal law (Art. 51) and that a specific moral or social motivation can be considered as an extenuating circumstance, reducing the terms of the punishment (Arts. 62 and 62bis). The evaluation of the judges is important in this regard. Cases concerning Muslims and religiously motivated crimes have dealt with forms of violence within the family (normally directed against women, both wives and daughters). A general prohibition of abuse and mistreatment is established by Article 572 of the Criminal Code; judges have not excluded the application of the criminal law, but two different positions have emerged.

---

2 Court of Cassation, criminal section, judgment 4 April 2006, n. 11919 (available at http://www.olir.it/documenti/?documento=3616, last accessed 29 January 2015).

3 Available at http://www.olir.it/documenti/?documento=1759 (last accessed 29 January 2015). The case concerned two children whose parents had performed respectively circumcision and infibulation. The sentence punished the parents on the basis of Arts. 582, 585, and 577of the Criminal Code, on bodily injuries. Another judgment is interesting at this regard, even if the circumcision was practised by a Christian family: Court of Cassation, n. 43646 of 24 November 2011 decided that the parents could not be considered liable because they had been deceived about the qualifications as a health professional of the person performing the circumcision (see http://www.olir.it/documenti/?documento=5722, last accessed 29 January 2015).

Case Law 1

The Court of Cassation considered irrelevant the cultural and religious motivations of acts of violence within the family and it did not apply any extenuating circumstance (Court of Cassation, criminal section, judgment 29 May 2009, n. 22700[4] and judgment 26 March 2009, n. 32824).[5]

Case Law 2

In another case, the Court of Cassation took into account the religious background of a father in the attempted murder of his daughter. The application of the criminal law was not excluded, but the terms of the sanction were decided without applying the aggravating circumstance of trivial motivations. The motivation for the attempted murder was, in fact, the father's knowledge of the behaviour of the daughter, who was not respecting Islamic law by having a relationship with a non-Muslim boyfriend (Court of Cassation, 18 December 2013, n. 51059).[6]

Codice penale 1930 (approvato con Regio Decreto 19 ottobre 1930, n. 1938). (as amended by legge 24 febbraio 2006, n. 85[7])

Art. 403. *Offese a una confessione religiosa mediante vilipendio di persone*
Chiunque pubblicamente offende una confessione religiosa, mediante vilipendio di chi la professa, è punito con la multa da euro 1.000 a euro 5.000.
Si applica la multa da euro 2.000 a euro 6.000 a chi offende una confessione religiosa, mediante vilipendio di un ministro di culto.

Art. 404. *Offese a una confessione religiosa mediante vilipendio o danneggiamento di cose*
Chiunque, in un luogo destinato al culto, o in un luogo pubblico o aperto al pubblico, offendendo una confessione religiosa, vilipende con espressioni ingiuriose cose che formino oggetto di culto, o siano consacrate al culto, o siano destinate necessariamente all'esercizio del culto, ovvero commette

4 Available at http://www.olir.it/documenti/?documento=5017 (last accessed 29 January 2015).
5 Available at http://www.olir.it/documenti/?documento=6466 (last accessed 29 January 2015).
6 Available at http://www.olir.it/documenti/?documento=6223 (last accessed 29 January 2015).
7 http://www.normattiva.it/uri-res/N2Ls?urn:nir:stato:legge:2006;85 (last accessed 29 January 2015).

il fatto in occasione di funzioni religiose, compiute in luogo privato da un ministro di culto, è punito con la multa da euro 1.000 a euro 5.000.
Chiunque pubblicamente e intenzionalmente distrugge, disperde, deteriora, rende inservibili o imbratta cose che formano oggetto di culto o siano consacrate al culto o destinate necessariamente all'esercizio del culto è punito con la reclusione fino a due anni.

Art. 405. *Turbamento di funzioni religiose del culto di una confessione religiosa*
Chiunque impedisce o turba l'esercizio di funzioni, cerimonie o pratiche religiose del culto di una confessione religiosa, la quali si compiano con l'assistenza di un ministro del culto medesimo o in un luogo destinato al culto, o in un luogo pubblico o aperto al pubblico, è punito con la reclusione fino a due anni.
Se concorrono fatti di violenza alle persone o di minaccia, si applica la reclusione da uno a tre anni.

Art. 724. *Bestemmia e manifestazioni oltraggiose verso i defunti*
Chiunque pubblicamente bestemmia, con invettive o parole oltraggiose, contro la Divinità è punito con la sanzione amministrativa pecuniaria da 51 euro a 309 euro.
La stessa sanzione si applica a chi compie qualsiasi pubblica manifestazione oltraggiosa verso i defunti.

Legge 13 ottobre 1975, n. 654. *Ratifica ed esecuzione della convenzione internazionale sull'eliminazione di tutte le forme di discriminazione razziale, aperta alla firma a New York il 7 marzo 1966*[8]

Art. 3
1. Salvo che il fatto costituisca più grave reato, anche ai fini dell'attuazione della disposizione dell'art. 4 della convenzione, è punito:
a) con la reclusione fino ad un anno e sei mesi o con la multa fino a 6.000 euro chi propaganda idee fondate sulla superiorità o sull'odio razziale o etnico, ovvero istiga a commettere o commette atti di discriminazione per motivi razziali, etnici, nazionali o religiosi;

---

8 As amended by decree law n. 122 of 26 April 1993, 'Misure urgenti in materia di discriminazione razziale, etnica e religiosa' (converted into Act n. 205 of 25 June 1993) and by Act n. 85 of 2006. The text in force is available at http://www.olir.it/documenti/?documento=1279, last accessed 29 January 2015.

b) con la reclusione da sei mesi a quattro anni chi, in qualsiasi modo, istiga a commettere o commette violenza o atti di provocazione alla violenza per motivi razziali, etnici, nazionali o religiosi
2. (soppresso)
3. È vietata ogni organizzazione, associazione, movimento o gruppo avente tra i propri scopi l'incitamento alla discriminazione o alla violenza per motivi razziali, etnici, nazionali o religiosi. Chi partecipa a tali organizzazioni, associazioni, movimenti o gruppi, o presta assistenza alla loro attività, è punito, per il solo fatto della partecipazione o dell'assistenza, con la reclusione da sei mesi a quattro anni. Coloro che promuovono o dirigono tali organizzazioni, associazioni, movimenti o gruppi sono puniti, per ciò solo, con la reclusione da uno a sei anni.

Legge 9 gennaio 2006, n. 7. ***Disposizioni concernenti la prevenzione e il divieto delle pratiche di mutilazione genitale femminile***
(GU n. 14 del 18-1-2006)[9]

Art. 1. *Finalità*
1. In attuazione degli articoli 2, 3 e 32 della Costituzione e di quanto sancito dalla Dichiarazione e dal Programma di azione adottati a Pechino il 15 settembre 1995 nella quarta Conferenza mondiale delle Nazioni Unite sulle donne, la presente legge detta le misure necessarie per prevenire, contrastare e reprimere le pratiche di mutilazione genitale femminile quali violazioni dei diritti fondamentali all'integrità della persona e alla salute delle donne e delle bambine.

Art. 2. *Attività di promozione e coordinamento*
1. La Presidenza del Consiglio dei ministri-Dipartimento per le pari opportunità promuove e sostiene, nell'ambito degli ordinari stanziamenti di bilancio, il coordinamento delle attività svolte dai Ministeri competenti dirette alla prevenzione, all'assistenza alle vittime e all'eliminazione delle pratiche di mutilazione genitale femminile.
2. Ai fini dello svolgimento delle attività di cui al comma 1, la Presidenza del Consiglio dei ministri-Dipartimento per le pari opportunità acquisisce dati e informazioni, a livello nazionale e internazionale, sull'attività svolta per la prevenzione e la repressione e sulle strategie di contrasto programmate o realizzate da altri Stati.

9 www.normattiva.it/uri-res/N2Ls?urn:nir:stato:legge:2006-01-09;7!vig=2015-02-02 (last accessed 2 February 2015).

Art. 3. *Campagne informative*
1. Allo scopo di prevenire e contrastare le pratiche di cui all'articolo 583-bis del codice penale, il Ministro per le pari opportunità, d'intesa con i Ministri della salute, dell'istruzione, dell'università e della ricerca, del lavoro e delle politiche sociali, degli affari esteri e dell'interno e con la Conferenza permanente per i rapporti tra lo Stato, le regioni e le province autonome di Trento e di Bolzano, predispone appositi programmi diretti a:
a) predisporre campagne informative rivolte agli immigrati dai Paesi in cui sono effettuate le pratiche di cui all'articolo 583-bis del codice penale, al momento della concessione del visto presso i consolati italiani e del loro arrivo alle frontiere italiane, dirette a diffondere la conoscenza dei diritti fondamentali della persona, in particolare delle donne e delle bambine, e del divieto vigente in Italia delle pratiche di mutilazione genitale femminile;
b) promuovere iniziative di sensibilizzazione, con la partecipazione delle organizzazioni di volontariato, delle organizzazioni no profit, delle strutture sanitarie, in particolare dei centri riconosciuti di eccellenza dall'Organizzazione mondiale della sanità, e con le comunità di immigrati provenienti dai Paesi dove sono praticate le mutilazioni genitali femminili per sviluppare l'integrazione socio-culturale nel rispetto dei diritti fondamentali della persona, in particolare delle donne e delle bambine;
c) organizzare corsi di informazione per le donne infibulate in stato di gravidanza, finalizzati ad una corretta preparazione al parto;
d) promuovere appositi programmi di aggiornamento per gli insegnanti delle scuole dell'obbligo, anche avvalendosi di figure di riconosciuta esperienza nel campo della mediazione culturale, per aiutarli a prevenire le mutilazioni genitali femminili, con il coinvolgimento dei genitori delle bambine e dei bambini immigrati, e per diffondere in classe la conoscenza dei diritti delle donne e delle bambine;
e) promuovere presso le strutture sanitarie e i servizi sociali il monitoraggio dei casi pregressi già noti e rilevati localmente.
[...]

Art. 4. *Formazione del personale sanitario*
1. Il Ministro della salute, sentiti i Ministri dell'istruzione, dell'università e della ricerca e per le pari opportunità e la Conferenza permanente per i rapporti tra lo Stato, le regioni e le province autonome di Trento e di Bolzano, emana, entro tre mesi dalla data di entrata in vigore della presente legge, linee guida destinate alle figure professionali sanitarie nonché ad altre figure professionali che operano con le comunità di immigrati provenienti da Paesi dove sono effettuate le pratiche di cui all'articolo 583-bis del codice penale per

realizzare un'attività di prevenzione, assistenza e riabilitazione delle donne e delle bambine già sottoposte a tali pratiche.

[...]

Art. 5. *Istituzione di un numero verde*

1. È istituito, entro tre mesi dalla data di entrata in vigore della presente legge, presso il Ministero dell'interno, un numero verde finalizzato a ricevere segnalazioni da parte di chiunque venga a conoscenza della effettuazione, sul territorio italiano, delle pratiche di cui all'articolo 583-bis del codice penale, nonché a fornire informazioni sulle organizzazioni di volontariato e sulle strutture sanitarie che operano presso le comunità di immigrati provenienti da Paesi dove sono effettuate tali pratiche.

[...]

Art. 6. *Pratiche di mutilazione degli organi genitali femminili*

1. Dopo l'articolo 583 del codice penale sono inseriti i seguenti:

«Art. 583-bis.—(Pratiche di mutilazione degli organi genitali femminili).—Chiunque, in assenza di esigenze terapeutiche, cagiona una mutilazione degli organi genitali femminili è punito con la reclusione da quattro a dodici anni. Ai fini del presente articolo, si intendono come pratiche di mutilazione degli organi genitali femminili la clitoridectomia, l'escissione e l'infibulazione e qualsiasi altra pratica che cagioni effetti dello stesso tipo.

Chiunque, in assenza di esigenze terapeutiche, provoca, al fine di menomare le funzioni sessuali, lesioni agli organi genitali femminili diverse da quelle indicate al primo comma, da cui derivi una malattia nel corpo o nella mente, è punito con la reclusione da tre a sette anni. La pena è diminuita fino a due terzi se la lesione è di lieve entità.

La pena è aumentata di un terzo quando le pratiche di cui al primo e al secondo comma sono commesse a danno di un minore ovvero se il fatto è commesso per fini di lucro.

Le disposizioni del presente articolo si applicano altresì quando il fatto è commesso all'estero da cittadino italiano o da straniero residente in Italia, ovvero in danno di cittadino italiano o di straniero residente in Italia. In tal caso, il colpevole è punito a richiesta del Ministro della giustizia.

Art. 583-ter.—(Pena accessoria).—La condanna contro l'esercente una professione sanitaria per taluno dei delitti previsti dall'articolo 583-bis importa la pena accessoria dell'interdizione dalla professione da tre a dieci anni. Della sentenza di condanna è data comunicazione all'Ordine dei medici chirurghi e degli odontoiatri».

[...]

Art. 7. *Programmi di cooperazione internazionale*
1. Nell'ambito dei programmi di cooperazione allo sviluppo condotti dal Ministero degli affari esteri e in particolare nei programmi finalizzati alla promozione dei diritti delle donne, in Paesi dove, anche in presenza di norme nazionali di divieto, continuano ad essere praticate mutilazioni genitali femminili, e comunque senza nuovi o maggiori oneri per lo Stato, sono previsti, in accordo con i Governi interessati, presso le popolazioni locali, progetti di formazione e informazione diretti a scoraggiare tali pratiche nonché a creare centri antiviolenza che possano eventualmente dare accoglienza alle giovani che intendano sottrarsi a tali pratiche ovvero alle donne che intendano sottrarvi le proprie figlie o le proprie parenti in età minore.

CHAPTER 15

Family Law

Article 29 of the Constitution recognises the right of the family as a natural society founded on marriage; paragraph 2 of the Article states the principle of equality between the spouses.

In Italy, there are different types of marriages: civil marriage, "concordatary" marriage (performed before a Catholic minister of religion, according to the Church–state agreement), religious marriage for religions with *intesa*, and religious marriage according to the legislation of 1929–1930, performed before an approved minister of religion. As long as Islam has no minister recognised by the state, Muslims cannot refer to the legislation of 1929–1930 in order to perform a religious marriage (see sect. 15.2). Legislation on private international law (sect. 15.1) is particularly relevant for Muslims because foreign residents form the majority of the Islamic community in Italy. Recognition of marriages performed abroad, as well as foreign family law, may emerge to define the status of Muslim residents in Italy or for family reunification procedures.

15.1 Private International Law

General rules on private international law were reformed in 1995. The main aspects of the applicable law, jurisdiction and procedural matters are included in Act n. 218 of 1995; some issues (for example marriages celebrated abroad) are regulated also in the Civil Code or other provisions.

With regard to civil status and family law, legislation in force determines some general conditions for the recognition of marriages celebrated abroad and for the celebration in Italy of marriages between foreign citizens.

For marriages celebrated abroad, the capacity to marry and the conditions for the celebration are normally regulated by the national law of the spouses. Foreign citizens can request the recognition in Italy of a marriage celebrated abroad, submitting the certificate of marriage (with its translation) to the Registrar's office or, in some cases, to the Consulate.[1] With regard to Muslim

1 This procedure and the rules on registration of acts of marriage are established by Decree of the President of the Republic (d.P.R.) n. 396 of 3 November 2000 ("*Semplificazione dell'ordinamento dello stato civile*"), especially in Arts. 10, 12, 16, 19 and 63. The decree regulates also the

foreign citizens, in some countries (for example Morocco) the spouses do not receive a proper marriage certificate, but a document declaring their existing union: in this case, registration in Italy can be achieved only if the consent to marriage of both parties can be demonstrated.[2]

In the case of foreigners formalising a marriage in Italy, Italian legislation (in particular the Civil Code, Art. 116, and Act n. 218 of 1995) establishes rules concerning capacity to marry, applicable law and procedures for the marriage of foreign citizens.[3] Foreign citizens enjoy the freedom to marry, and they have to follow the Italian rules and procedures to conclude a valid marriage.

The rules of private international law determine the application of the law of the nationality in various aspects of civil status, such as the capacity to marry and impediments. In this area, Italian legislation does not make express reference to the application of religious laws, even if Islamic principles are the source of some foreign state's applicable legislation. Cases of recognition of marriages (including religious unions) celebrated abroad are regulated as a relation between the legislations of two states. In this regard, Article 16 of d.P.R. n. 200 of 1967 (no longer in force) established that a religious marriage performed abroad could be registered as a civil marriage in Italy when it had civil effects also in the foreign country. In any case, as a general principle, Article 16 of Act n. 218 of 1995 states that no foreign provision can be applied in Italy when it is in conflict with the principle of public order. Monitoring compliance with this principle—and with the fundamental principles of the Italian legal order—can imply verification also of religious aspects of foreign acts, as we can see through the analysis of the jurisprudence.[4]

---

banns of marriage, at Arts. 50–58 (available at www.normattiva.it/uri-res/N2Ls?urn:nir:stato:decreto.del.presidente.della.repubblica:2000-11-03;396!vig=2015-01-23, last accessed 23 January 2015). For citizens of some countries the requirements for the registration of marriage certificates or for the celebration of marriage in Italy are different, depending on the ratification of some international conventions on cooperation in matters of civil status (for example the Convention of Munich, 5 September 1980, ratified in Italy by Act n. 950 of 1984). Rules are different, obviously, for citizens of the EU Member States.

2 See circular n. 25 of the Ministry of the Interior, 13 October 2011 (available at http://www.stranieriinitalia.it/images/circ013ott2011.pdf, last accessed 23 January 2015).

3 See also d.P.R. n. 369 of 2000, cit.

4 For other cases and further analysis on this issue see Campiglio, Cristina, 'Il diritto di famiglia islamico nella prassi italiana', *Rivista di diritto internazionale privato e processuale* (no. 1, 2008), pp. 43–76.

Case Law

The Council of State (Consiglio di Stato, sez. III, decision 7 June 1988 n. 640[5]) affirmed that Islamic law connects to marriage some goals that are not very different from the nature and aims of marriage celebrated in Italy; therefore, a marriage performed abroad according to Islamic rites can be transcribed into the registers of Italian civil status if it has civil relevance in the foreign country. The public officer shall verify that there are no substantive elements in conflict with Italian fundamental principles by means of an examination of the presence of impediments. For example, the free state of both spouses shall be verified, and the transcription will be denied if the marriage is the second union of a polygamist. Tribunals have confirmed the validity of marriage performed abroad following Islamic law (for example Court of Cassation, judgment n. 1739 of 2 March 1999;[6] Tribunal of Milan, decision 2 February 2007[7]) in so far as Italian public order is respected.[8]

Codice civile[9]
(Regio decreto 16 marzo 1942, n. 262, *Approvazione del testo del Codice civile*)

Art. 116
Lo straniero che vuole contrarre matrimonio nello Stato deve presentare all'ufficiale dello stato civile una dichiarazione dell'autorità competente del proprio paese, dalla quale risulti che giusta le leggi a cui è sottoposto nulla osta al matrimonio.
Anche lo straniero è tuttavia soggetto alle disposizioni contenute negli articoli 85, 86, 87, numeri, 1, 2 e 4, 88 e 89.

5 Published in *Servizi demografici*, 1988, p. 74.

6 http://www.olir.it/documenti/?documento=6470 (last accessed 3 February 2015).

7 http://www.olir.it/documenti/?documento=4174 (last accessed 23 January 2015). In this case the marriage had been performed by telephone and considered valid under Pakistani legislation; it can be declared valid also in Italy, according to Art. 28 of Act n. 218 of 1995.

8 See also ministerial Circular MIACEL n. 2/2001 of 26 March 2001, which specifies that, in the case of an Islamic marriage which is a polygamous union, only the first marriage can be registered in Italy with civil effects, as long as polygamy is in conflict with public order. The text of the circular is available at http://www.immigrazione.regione.toscana.it/lenya/paesi/live/contenuti/norme/circolare-2-2001.html?datafine=20150123# (last accessed 23 January 2015).

9 http://www.normattiva.it/uri-res/N2Ls?urn:nir:stato:regio.decreto:1942-03-16;262 (last accessed 23 January 2015).

Lo straniero che ha domicilio o residenza nello Stato deve inoltre far fare la pubblicazione secondo le disposizioni di questo codice.

Legge 31 maggio 1995, n. 218. *Riforma del Sistema italiano di diritto internazionale privato*[10]

Art. 1. *Oggetto della legge*
1. La presente legge determina l'ambito della giurisdizione italiana, pone i criteri per l'individuazione del diritto applicabile e disciplina l'efficacia delle sentenze e degli atti stranieri.

Art. 2. *Convenzioni internazionali*
1. Le disposizioni della presente legge non pregiudicano l'applicazione delle convenzioni internazionali in vigore per l'Italia.
2. Nell'interpretazione di tali convenzioni si terrà conto del loro carattere internazionale e dell'esigenza della loro applicazione uniforme.

Art. 3. *Ambito della giurisdizione*
1. La giurisdizione italiana sussiste quando il convenuto è domiciliato o residente in Italia o vi ha un rappresentante che sia autorizzato a stare in giudizio a norma dell'articolo 77 del codice di procedura civile e negli altri casi in cui è prevista dalla legge.
2. La giurisdizione sussiste inoltre in base ai criteri stabiliti dalle sezioni 2, 3 e 4 del titolo II della Convenzione concernente la competenza giurisdizionale e l'esecuzione delle decisioni in materia civile e commerciale e protocollo, firmati a Bruxelles il 27 settembre 1968, resi esecutivi con la legge 21 giugno 1971, n. 804, e successive modificazioni in vigore per l'Italia, anche allorché il convenuto non sia domiciliato nel territorio di uno Stato contraente, quando si tratti di una delle materie comprese nel campo di applicazione della Convenzione. Rispetto alle altre materie la giurisdizione sussiste anche in base ai criteri stabiliti per la competenza per territorio.
[...]

10 www.normattiva.it/uri-res/N2Ls?urn:nir:stato:legge:1995-05-31;218!vig=2015-01-23 (last accessed 23 January 2015).

Art. 6. *Questioni preliminari*
1. Il giudice italiano conosce, incidentalmente, le questioni che non rientrano nella giurisdizione italiana e la cui soluzione è necessaria per decidere sulla domanda proposta.

Art. 7. *Pendenza di un processo straniero*
1. Quando, nel corso del giudizio, sia eccepita la previa pendenza tra le stesse parti didomanda avente il medesimo oggetto e il medesimo titolo dinanzi a un giudice straniero, il giudice italiano, se ritiene che il provvedimento straniero possa produrre effetto per l'ordinamento italiano, sospende il giudizio. Se il giudice straniero declina la propria giurisdizione o se il provvedimento straniero non è riconosciuto nell'ordinamento italiano, il giudizio in Italia prosegue, previa riassunzione ad istanza della parte interessata.
2. La pendenza della causa innanzi al giudice straniero si determina secondo la legge dello Stato in cui il processo si svolge.
3. Nel caso di pregiudizialità di una causa straniera, il giudice italiano può sospendere il processo se ritiene che il provvedimento straniero possa produrre effetti per l'ordinamento italiano.
[...]

Art. 9. *Giurisdizione volontaria*
1. In materia di giurisdizione volontaria, la giurisdizione sussiste, oltre che nei casi specificamente contemplati dalla presente legge e in quelli in cui è prevista la competenza per territorio di un giudice italiano, quando il provvedimento richiesto concerne un cittadino italiano o una persona residente in Italia o quando esso riguarda situazioni o rapporti ai quali è applicabile la legge italiana.
[...]

Art. 13. *Rinvio*
1. Quando negli articoli successivi è richiamata la legge straniera, si tiene conto del rinvio operato dal diritto internazionale privato straniero alla legge di un altro Stato:
a) se il diritto di tale Stato accetta il rinvio;
b) se si tratta di rinvio alla legge italiana.
2. L'applicazione del comma 1 è tuttavia esclusa:
a) nei casi in cui le disposizioni della presente legge rendono applicabile la legge straniera sulla base della scelta effettuata in tal senso dalle parti interessate;
b) riguardo alle disposizioni concernenti la forma degli atti;

c) in relazione alle disposizioni del Capo XI del presente Titolo.
3. Nei casi di cui agli articoli 33, 34 e 35 si tiene conto del rinvio soltanto se esso conduce all'applicazione di una legge che consente lo stabilimento della filiazione.
4. Quando la presente legge dichiara in ogni caso applicabile una convenzione internazionale si segue sempre, in materia di rinvio, la soluzione adottata dalla convenzione.

Art. 14. *Conoscenza della legge straniera applicabile*
1. L'accertamento della legge straniera è compiuto d'ufficio dal giudice. A tal fine questi può avvalersi, oltre che degli strumenti indicati dalle convenzioni internazionali, di informazioni acquisite per il tramite del Ministero di grazia e giustizia; può altresì interpellare esperti o istituzioni specializzate.
2. Qualora il giudice non riesca ad accertare la legge straniera indicata, neanche con l'aiuto delle parti, applica la legge richiamata mediante altri criteri di collegamento eventualmente previsti per la medesima ipotesi normativa. In mancanza si applica la legge italiana.
[...]

Art. 16. *Ordine pubblico*
1. La legge straniera non è applicata se i suoi effetti sono contrari all'ordine pubblico.
2. In tal caso si applica la legge richiamata mediante altri criteri di collegamento eventualmente previsti per la medesima ipotesi normativa. In mancanza si applica la legge italiana.
[...]

Art. 18. *Ordinamenti plurilegislativi*
1. Se nell'ordinamento dello Stato richiamato dalle disposizioni della presente legge coesistono più sistemi normativi a base territoriale o personale, la legge applicabile si determina secondo i criteri utilizzati da quell'ordinamento.
2. Se tali criteri non possono essere individuati, si applica il sistema normativo con il quale il caso di specie presenta il collegamento più stretto.
[...]

Art. 27. *Condizioni per contrarre matrimonio*
1. La capacità matrimoniale e le altre condizioni per contrarre matrimonio sono regolate dalla legge nazionale di ciascun nubendo al momento del matrimonio. Resta salvo lo stato libero che uno dei nubendi abbia acquistato per effetto di un giudicato italiano o riconosciuto in Italia.

Art. 28. *Forma del matrimonio*
1. Il matrimonio è valido, quanto alla forma, se è considerato tale dalla legge del luogo di celebrazione o dalla legge nazionale di almeno uno dei coniugi al momento della celebrazione o dalla legge dello Stato di comune residenza in tale momento.

Art. 29. *Rapporti personali tra coniugi*
1. I rapporti personali tra coniugi sono regolati dalla legge nazionale comune.
2. I rapporti personali tra coniugi aventi diverse cittadinanze o più cittadinanze comuni sono regolati dalla legge dello Stato nel quale la vita matrimoniale è prevalentemente localizzata.
[...]

Art. 31. *Separazione personale e scioglimento del matrimonio*
1. La separazione personale e lo scioglimento del matrimonio sono regolati dalla legge nazionale comune dei coniugi al momento della domanda di separazione o di scioglimento del matrimonio; in mancanza si applica la legge dello Stato nel quale la vita matrimoniale risulta prevalentemente localizzata.
2. La separazione personale e lo scioglimento del matrimonio, qualora non siano previsti dalla legge straniera applicabile, sono regolati dalla legge italiana.

Art. 32. *Giurisdizione in materia di nullità, annullamento, separazione personale e scioglimento del matrimonio*
1. In materia di nullità e di annullamento del matrimonio, di separazione personale e di scioglimento del matrimonio, la giurisdizione italiana sussiste, oltre che nei casi previsti dall'articolo 3, anche quando uno dei coniugi è cittadino italiano o il matrimonio è stato celebrato in Italia.

Decreto del Presidente della Repubblica 3 novembre 2000 n. 396. *Regolamento per la revisione e la semplificazione dell'ordinamento dello stato civile, a norma dell'articolo 2, comma 12, della legge 15 maggio 1997, n. 127*
(GU n. 303 del 30-12-2000—Suppl. Ordinario n. 223)[11]

11 http://www.normattiva.it/uri-res/N2Ls?urn:nir:stato:decreto.del.presidente.della .repubblica:2000-11-03;396 (last accessed 23 January 2015).

Art. 16 *Matrimonio celebrato all'estero*
1. Il matrimonio all'estero, quando gli sposi sono entrambi cittadini italiani o uno di essi è cittadino italiano e l'altro è cittadino straniero, può essere celebrato innanzi all'autorità diplomatica o consolare competente, oppure innanzi all'autorità locale secondo le leggi del luogo. In quest'ultimo caso una copia dell'atto è rimessa a cura degli interessati all'autorità diplomatica o consolare.

Art. 19. *Trascrizioni*
1. Su richiesta dei cittadini stranieri residenti in Italia possono essere trascritti, nel comune dove essi risiedono, gli atti dello stato civile che li riguardano formati all'estero. Tali atti devono essere presentati unitamente alla traduzione in lingua italiana e alla legalizzazione, ove prescritta, da parte della competente autorità straniera.
2. Possono altresì essere trascritti gli atti dei matrimoni celebrati fra cittadini stranieri dinanzi all'autorità diplomatica o consolare straniera in Italia, se ciò è consentito dalle convenzioni vigenti in materia con il Paese cui detta autorità appartiene.
3. L'ufficiale dello stato civile può rilasciare copia integrale dell'atto trascritto a richiesta degli interessati.

Art. 63. *Iscrizioni e trascrizioni*
1. Negli archivi di cui all'articolo 10, l'ufficiale dello stato civile iscrive:
[...]
2. Nei medesimi archivi l'ufficiale dello stato civile trascrive:
c) gli atti dei matrimoni celebrati all'estero;
d) gli atti dei matrimoni celebrati dinanzi all'autorità diplomatica o consolare straniera in Italia fra cittadini stranieri quando esistono convenzioni in materia;
[...]
f) le sentenze dalle quali risulta la esistenza del matrimonio;
g) le sentenze e gli altri atti con cui si pronuncia all'estero la nullità, lo scioglimento, la cessazione degli effetti civili di un matrimonio ovvero si rettifica in qualsiasi modo un atto di matrimonio già iscritto o trascritto negli archivi di cui all'articolo 10;
[...]

15.2 Marriage and Divorce

In Italy, recognition of the civil effects of religious marriages is possible, but only for religious denominations that have signed an agreement with the state: the Concordat of 1984 introduced a concordat-based marriage for Catholics, and the agreements (*intese*) with other religious denominations allow the celebration of religious marriages and their civil recognition. For denominations with no *intesa*—such as Islam—Act n. 1159 of 1929 establishes that a religious marriage can have the effects of a civil marriage when it is performed before a minister of religion who has been approved by the state in accordance with Article 3 of the Act (see above, sect. 1.5).[12] As no minister of Islamic religion has been recognised under Act n. 1159 of 1929, this procedure is not currently applicable. A marriage celebrated in Italy with Islamic ritual (for example celebration in a mosque) is not valid,[13] even if a mere religious marriage is not in itself prohibited by the legislation in force. Some effects of mere religious unions can be recognised, for example with regard to filiation matters. The presence (and effects) of such unregistered religious marriages has posed the problem of controlling some consequences and characteristics that may be contrary to the Italian legal order, e.g. gender inequality, arranged and forced marriages, polygamy and repudiation.

With regard to gender inequality, Article 29.2 of the Italian Constitution states that the spouses are equal both from a legal and from a moral point of view. The partners have the same rights and the same position; the Italian legal system gives great importance to the freedom of choice with regard to marriage. A peculiarity of Islamic marriage is that it excludes marriages between a Muslim woman and a non-Muslim man. Therefore, if a foreign woman living in Italy intends to celebrate marriage with a non-Muslim, she will need permission from the Consulate of the country of origin stating that there is no impediment to the marriage (*nulla-osta*). There have been cases where such permission was denied: both case law and a circular of the Ministry of the

---

12 Article 11 of Act n. 1159/1929 specifies that, in any case, when a marriage is performed before a minister of an "admitted cult", it is entirely regulated by the legislation on civil marriage, for example with regard to the discipline of the relations between the spouses and to the causes of annulment or dissolution of marriage.

13 See decision of the Regional Administrative Tribunal of Piemonte (TAR Piemonte) of 23 October 2006, n. 3728: it is not possible to demand the recognition of a Muslim marriage celebrated in Italy, in so far as it is not performed before an approved minister of religion (available at http://www.olir.it/documenti/?documento=4018, last accessed 23 January 2015).

Interior have stated that Italy grants the full freedom to marry to both parties, thus that permit was declared unnecessary.[14]

With regard to forced marriage, there is no specific legislation on this issue: Articles on private violence (Art. 610 of the Criminal Code), menace (Art. 612 of the Criminal Code) and on violence to extort consent to marry (Art. 122 of the Civil Code) may be used. As mentioned above (sect. 14), there are cases where the principle of gender equality is not respected, or relationships with the offspring caused violence within the family (for example there are cases where parents force children in the choice of a partner). In such situations criminal law may be applied.

Polygamy is illegal in Italy. Article 86 of the Civil Code establishes that marriage is invalid if one of the spouses is already married, and Article 556 of the Criminal Code criminalises the conduct of a person who, already bound in marriage, celebrated another marriage. A note from the Ministry of the Exterior has excluded the civil effects of a polygamous union in cases where the spouses want to obtain visas or residence permits;[15] similarly, the National Pension Agency has reiterated that the family maintenance policy cannot take into account more than one spouse.[16] However, some effects of polygamous unions are recognised, particularly with regard to filiation. For example, there are cases where children born in a polygamous marriage were authorised to enter Italy through the family reunification procedure, even if only one wife is normally authorised.[17] Other indirect effects of polygamy concern inheritance matters.[18]

---

14 See Circular of the Ministry of the Interior, 11 September 2007, n. 46.

15 Message of 21 August 2009, 'Legge n. 94/09—Modifiche al T.U. n. 286/98' (about Act n. 94/09 amending d.lgs. n. 286/98 on immigration, available at http://www.olir.it/documenti/?documento=5162, last accessed 23 January 2015).

16 INPS (National Pension Agency): message of 29 September 2006, n. 25928, 'Assegno per il nucleo familiare in caso di poligamia' (on family maintenance policy in case of polygamy, available at http://www.olir.it/documenti/?documento=3927, last accessed 23 January 2015).

17 See the case law below. For further analysis see Petralia, Valentina, 'Ricongiungimento familiare e matrimonio poligamico. Il riconoscimento di valori giuridici stranieri e la tutela delle posizioni deboli', *Università di Catania—Online Working Paper*, 2013, no. 49, at http://www.cde.unict.it/sites/default/files/Quaderno%20europeo_49_febbraio_2013.pdf (last accessed 20 May 2015); Durisotto, David, 'Poligamia e ordinamenti europei', in Cardia, Carlo and Dalla Torre, Giuseppe, *Comunità islamiche in Italia. Identità e forme giuridiche*, pp. 357 ff.

18 See the cases and analysis in Rocchini, Ylenia, 'Matrimonio poligamico islamico e famiglie immigrate: l'esperienza giurisprudenziale italiana tra diritto privato e diritto pubblico', in Amram, Denise, and D'Angelo, Angela (eds), *La famiglia e il diritto fra diversità nazionali ed iniziative dell'Unione Europea* (Padova: Cedam, 2011), pp. 279–300.

With regard to repudiation, in Italy this is not a recognised divorce practice. There have been cases concerning the recognition of decisions of a foreign state on this matter. The fundamental principle to be followed is that a decision on marriage dissolution can be recognised in Italy if it is consistent with public order (according to the international private law criteria, as already said in sect. 15.1).

Case Law

With regard to polygamy, the Court of Appeal of Turin (decree 18 April 2001[19]) authorised a temporary visa to the second wife of a Moroccan citizen living in Italy in order to give her the opportunity of taking care of her child who was already in Italy with the father. In this case, and in other similar hypotheses, judges normally follow the principle of the best interest of the child.

With regard to repudiation, judges of the tribunal of Milan declared it contrary to Italian public order; therefore, repudiation cannot be recognised as a civil decree of divorce.[20] Another court gave civil effects to a foreign act of repudiation (*talaq*), in so far as some essential rights were granted, such as the possibility of both parties to intervene in the procedure of separation (Court of Appeal of Cagliari, decision n. 198 of 2008).[21]

Costituzione

Art. 29.
1. La Repubblica riconosce i diritti della famiglia come società naturale fondata sul matrimonio.
2. Il matrimonio è ordinato sull'eguaglianza morale e giuridica dei coniugi, con i limiti stabiliti dalla legge a garanzia dell'unità familiare.

Legge 24 giugno 1929, n. 1159: *Disposizioni sull'esercizio dei culti ammessi nello Stato e sul matrimonio celebrato davanti ai ministri dei culti medesimi.*

19 See the text in "Diritto di famiglia", 2001, 1492 ff.

20 Civil Tribunal (Tribunale Civile) of Milano, decision n. 3327 of 24 March 1994 (available at http://www.olir.it/documenti/?documento=963, last accessed 23 January 2015).

21 Court of Appeal (Corte d'Appello) of Cagliari, decision n. 198 of 16 May 2008 (available at http://www.stranieriinitalia.it/briguglio/immigrazione-e-asilo/2008/settembre/sent-corte-app-ca-talaq.html, last accessed 23 January 2015).

Art. 7
Il matrimonio celebrato davanti ad alcuno dei ministri di culto indicati nel precedente art. 3 produce dal giorno della celebrazione gli stessi effetti del matrimonio celebrato davanti l'ufficiale dello stato civile, quando siano osservate le disposizioni degli articoli seguenti.

Art. 8
Chi intende celebrare il matrimonio davanti alcuno dei ministri di culto, indicati nel precedente art. 3, deve dichiararlo all'ufficiale di stato civile, che sarebbe competente a celebrare il matrimonio. L'ufficiale dello stato civile, dopo che siano state adempiute tutte le formalità preliminari e, dopo avere accertato che nulla si oppone alla celebrazione del matrimonio secondo le norme del codice civile, rilascia autorizzazione scritta con indicazione del ministro del culto davanti al quale la celebrazione deve aver luogo e della data del provvedimento, con cui la nomina di questi venne approvata a' termini dell'art. 3.

Art. 9
Il ministro del culto, davanti al quale avviene la celebrazione, deve dare lettura agli sposi degli artt. 130, 131 e 132 del codice civile[22] e ricevere, alla presenza di due testimoni idonei, la dichiarazione espressa di entrambi gli sposi, l'uno dopo l'altro, di volersi prendere rispettivamente in marito e moglie, osservata la disposizione dell'art. 95 del codice civile. L'atto di matrimonio dev'essere compilato immediatamente dopo la celebrazione, redatto in lingua italiana nelle forme stabilite dagli artt. 352 e 353 del codice civile per gli atti dello stato civile e deve contenere le indicazioni richieste nell'art. 10 della presente legge. L'atto, così compilato, sarà subito trasmesso in originale all'ufficiale dello stato civile e, in ogni caso, non oltre cinque giorni dalla celebrazione.

Art. 10
L'ufficiale dello stato civile, ricevuto l'atto di matrimonio, ne cura, entro le ventiquattro ore, la trascrizione nei registri dello stato civile, in modo che risultino le seguenti indicazioni: il nome e cognome, l'età e la professione, il luogo di nascita, il domicilio o la residenza degli sposi; il nome e cognome, il domicilio o la residenza dei loro genitori; la data delle eseguite pubblicazioni o il decreto di dispensa; la data del decreto di dispensa, ove sia stata concessa, da alcuno degli impedimenti di legge; il luogo e la data in cui seguì la celebra-

22 Now Arts. 143, 144 and 147 of the Civil Code.

zione del matrimonio; il nome e cognome del ministro del culto dinanzi al quale seguì la celebrazione del matrimonio. L'ufficiale dello stato civile deve dare avviso al procuratore della Repubblica, nei casi e per gli effetti indicati nell'art. 104 del R.D. 15 novembre 1865, n. 2602, per l'ordinamento dello stato civile.

Art. 11
Al matrimonio celebrato davanti il ministro di un culto ammesso nello Stato e debitamente trascritto nei registri dello stato civile si applicano, anche per quanto riguarda le domande di nullità, tutte le disposizioni riflettenti il matrimonio celebrato davanti l'ufficiale dello stato civile.

Art. 12
Agli effetti dell'art. 124 codice civile è parificato alla celebrazione del matrimonio il rilascio dell'autorizzazione prevista nell'art. 8 della presente legge. Incorre nella multa stabilita nell'art. 124 del codice civile l'ufficiale dello stato civile che omette di eseguire la trascrizione dell'atto di matrimonio, entro il termine indicato nell'art. 10 della presente legge.

Regio Decreto 28 febbraio 1930, n. 289. ***Norme per l'attuazione della legge 24 giugno 1929, n. 1159/1929, sui culti ammessi nello Stato e per il coordinamento di essa con le altre leggi dello Stato***

Art. 25
L'autorizzazione che l'ufficiale dello stato civile rilascia, a termini dell'art. 8 della legge, al ministro di un culto diverso dalla religione cattolica per la celebrazione di un matrimonio, comprende la facoltà del ministro stesso di delegare, in caso di legittimo impedimento il ministro di culto che legalmente lo sostituisce nell'ufficio, se però la nomina del medesimo è stata debitamente approvata ai sensi dell'art. 3 della legge.
Nella delega, che deve essere fatta per iscritto, il ministro delegante deve far menzione dell'autorizzazione ricevuta e dell'impedimento sopravvenuto e deve indicare il ministro delegato e la data del provvedimento di approvazione della nomina dello stesso.
L'atto di delega deve essere allegato all'originale dell'atto di matrimonio da trasmettersi all'ufficiale dello stato civile.

Art. 26
Se gli sposi domiciliano o risiedono in comune diverso da quello di residenza del ministro di culto, innanzi al quale intendono celebrare il matrimonio, e

si trasferiscono in questo ultimo comune per la celebrazione, l'ufficiale dello stato civile della loro residenza richiede della celebrazione del matrimonio l'ufficiale dello stato civile del comune di residenza del ministro di culto e l'autorizzazione di cui all'articolo precedente è data da quest'ultimo ufficiale di stato civile.
Se invece, il ministro di culto si trasferisce nel comune del domicilio o della residenza degli sposi per celebrare il matrimonio, l'autorizzazione gli è data dall'ufficiale dello stato civile del comune stesso, dopo che si sarà fatto conoscere al medesimo con la esibizione degli occorrenti documenti e della copia del provvedimento di approvazione della sua nomina, a sensi dell'art. 3 della legge.

Art. 27
La trasmissione dell'originale dell'atto di matrimonio è fatta dal ministro di culto che lo celebra all'ufficiale dello stato civile da cui fu rilasciata la relativa autorizzazione. Della ricezione dell'atto dev'essere data assicurazione al mittente.
Nel caso previsto dal primo comma dell'articolo precedente l'ufficiale dello stato civile che rilasciò l'autorizzazione trasmette copia autentica dell'atto all'ufficiale da cui venne la richiesta.
Avvenuta la trascrizione dell'atto di matrimonio nel registro dello stato civile, l'ufficiale che vi procedette ne dà notizia, con l'indicazione della data in cui avvenne, al ministro di culto che celebrò il matrimonio.
In margine dei registri di matrimonio, parte II, serie A, deve prendersi nota della trasmissione di tale notizia.

15.3 Children

The Civil Code regulates the main aspects concerning filiation, parental authority, status of a minor; some issues are regulated by specific pieces of legislation, for example Act n. 184 of 4 May 1983 on adoption. These rules do not refer to religious aspects; in courts' decisions, sometimes the religious affiliation of parents has been considered in the adjudication of parental authority.[23]

Jurisprudence has also been the source of recognition of *kafalah* as a form of adoption, with effects in the Italian legal order (e.g. in decisions about family

23 There are no cases about Islam.

reunification: Court of Cassation, judgments n. 21108 of 16 September 2013;[24] n. 7472 of 20 March 2008[25]). In some cases, however, *kafalah* has not been considered as a proper adoption according to Italian legislation: it implies the duty of custody of the child but it does not give rise to the full legal authority of the *kafil* parent (Court of Cassation, judgment n. 21395 of 4 November 2005[26]). In another recent case, the Court of Cassation denied a family reunification visa for a child adopted by *kafalah* (judgment n. 4868 of 1 March 2010[27]).

With regard to some practices concerning children, while female genital mutilation is prohibited by Italian criminal law (see above, ch. 14), male circumcision is admitted. A decree of the President of the Council of Ministers of 2001 excluded circumcision from the operations that are performed at the expense of the National Health Service. Some local provisions have reaffirmed that principle, establishing in detail the conditions for that practice, in the context of the regional health service.[28]

Decreto del Presidente del Consiglio dei Ministri del 29 novembre 2001. *Definizione dei livelli essenziali di assistenza.*
(Da Supplemento ordinario n. 26 alla "Gazzetta Ufficiale della Repubblica Italiana" n. 33 dell'8 febbraio 2001)[29]

Art. 1.
1. Il presente decreto definisce, ai sensi dell'articolo 1 del decreto legislativo 30 dicembre 1992, n. 502, e successive modificazioni e integrazioni, e dell'articolo 6 del decreto-legge 18 settembre 2001, n. 347, convertito, con modificazioni, dalla legge 16 novembre 2001, n. 405, e conformemente agli Accordi fra il Governo, le Regioni e le Province autonome di Trento e di Bolzano sanciti dalla Conferenza permanente per il rapporti fra lo Stato, le Regioni e le Province autonome di Trento e di Bolzano in data 8 agosto e 22 novembre 2001, i livelli essenziali di assistenza sanitaria di cui agli allegati 1, 2, 3 e 3.1 che costituiscono parte integrante del presente decreto e alle linee-guida di cui all'allegato 4.

24 http://www.olir.it/documenti/?documento=6171 (last accessed 23 January 2015).
25 http://www.olir.it/documenti/?documento=4612 (last accessed 23 January 2015).
26 http://www.olir.it/documenti/?documento=3975 (last accessed 23 January 2015).
27 http://www.olir.it/documenti/?documento=5599 (last accessed 20 May 2015).
28 For example, the deliberation of the Piemonte Region, n. 49–12479 of 2 November 2009 ("Aggiornamento del nomenclatore tariffario regionale delle prestazioni di assistenza specialistica ambulatoriale—D.G.R. n. 73–13176 del 26.07.2004 e s.m.i.—ed ulteriori indicazioni, available at http://www.olir.it/documenti/?documento=5720, last accessed 23 January 2015).
29 http://www.olir.it/documenti/?documento=1743 (last accessed 20 May 2015).

[...]

All. 2. Allegato 2A
Prestazioni totalmente escluse dai LEA:
a) chirurgia estetica non conseguente ad incidenti, malattie o malformazioni congenite;
b) circoncisione rituale maschile;
[...]

Bibliography

Alicino, Francesco, "Imams and other Religious Authorities in Italy", *Stato, Chiese e Pluralismo confessionale*, 12 January 2015 (online journal, at www.statoechiese.it).

Alicino, Francesco, *La legislazione sulla base di intesa. I test delle religioni 'altre' e degli ateismi*, Bari: Cacucci, 2013.

Allievi, Stefano, "Immigration, religious diversity and recognition of differences: the Italian way to multiculturalism", *Identities: Global Studies in Culture and Power*, 21:6 (2014), pp. 724–737.

Allievi, Stefano, *Conflicts over Mosques in Europe. Policy issues and trends*, London: Alliance Publishing Trust, 2009 (at http://www.nef-europe.org/wp-content/uploads/2013/03/Conflicts-over-mosques_NEF-RelDem-RELIGION-MOSQUES-Final-1.pdf).

Allievi, Stefano (ed.), *I musulmani e la società italiana. Percezioni reciproche, conflitti culturali, trasformazioni sociali*, Milan: Franco Angeli, 2009.

Allievi, Stefano, *Islam italiano. Viaggio nella seconda religione del paese*, Turin: Einaudi 2003.

Allievi, Stefano, "Sociology of a Newcomer: Muslim Migration to Italy—Religious Visibility, Cultural and Political Reactions", *Immigrants & Minorities: Historical Studies in Ethnicity, Migration and Diaspora*, 22:2–3 (2003), pp. 141–154.

Allievi, Stefano, "Muslims in Italy", in Leveau, Rémy, Mohsen-Finan, Khadija, and Wihtol de Wenden, Catherine (eds), *New European Identity and Citizenship*, Farnham: Ashgate 2002, pp. 37–47.

Allievi, Stefano, "Muslim Organizations and Islam-State Relations: The Italian Case", in Shadid, Wasif A.R., and Sjoerd van Koningsveld, P. (eds), *Muslims in the Margin*, Kampen: KOK Pharos, 1996, pp. 182–201.

Allievi, Stefano, and Castro, Francesco, "The Islamic Presence in Italy: Social Rootedness and Legal Questions", in Ferrari, Silvio, and Bradney, Anthony (eds), *Islam and European Legal Systems*, Farnham: Ashgate, 2000, pp. 155–180.

Aluffi Beck-Peccoz, Roberta, "The Legal Treatment of the Muslim Minority in Italy", in Aluffi Beck-Peccoz, Roberta, and Zincone, Giovanna, *The Legal Treatment of Islamic Minorities in Europe*, Leuven: Peeters, 2004, pp. 133–157.

Angelucci, Antonio, "L'Albo delle associazioni e organizzazioni religiose del Comune di Milano", *Quaderni di diritto e politica ecclesiastica*, 2013, no. 2, pp. 461–478.

Angelucci, Antonio, Bombardieri, Maria, and Tacchini, Davide (eds), *Islam e integrazione in Italia*, Venice: Marsilio, 2014.

Basile, Fabio, "Società multiculturali, immigrazione e reati culturalmente motivati (comprese le mutilazioni genitali femminili)", *Stato, Chiese e Pluralismo confessionale*, October 2007 (online journal, at www.statoechiese.it).

Bombardieri, Maria, *Moschee d'Italia. Il diritto al luogo di culto. Il dibattito sociale e politico*, Bologna: EMI, 2011.

Campiglio, Cristina, "Il diritto di famiglia islamico nella prassi italiana", *Rivista di diritto internazionale privato e processuale*, 2008, n. 1, pp. 43–76.

Cardia, Carlo, and Dalla Torre, Giuseppe (eds.), *Comunità islamiche in Italia. Identità e forme giuridiche*, Turin: Giappichelli Editore, 2015.

Cardia, Carlo, "Carta dei valori e multiculturalità alla prova della Costituzione", *Stato, Chiese e Pluralismo confessionale*, 15 December 2008, (online journal, at www.statoechiese.it).

Casuscelli, Giuseppe, "La libertà religiosa alla prova dell'Islām: la peste dell'intolleranza", in Aluffi Beck-Peccoz, Roberta (ed.), *Identità religiosa e integrazione dei musulmani in Italia e in Europa. Omaggio alla memoria di Francesco Castro*, Turin: Giappichelli, 2008, pp. 53–70.

Casuscelli, Giuseppe (ed.), *Nozioni di Diritto ecclesiastico*, Turin: Giappichelli, 2015.

Chizzoniti, Antonio G., "La tutela della diversità: cibo, diritto e religione", in Chizzoniti, Antonio G., and Tallacchini, Mariachiara (eds), *Cibo e religione: diritto e diritti*, Tricase (Le): Libellula Edizioni, 2010, pp. 19–46.

Cilardo, Agostino, *Il diritto islamico e il sistema giuridico italiano. Le bozze di intesa tra la Repubblica italiana e le associazioni islamiche italiane*, Naples: ESI, 2002.

Ciotola, Claudia, "La legge sul divieto delle pratiche di mutilazione genitale femminile", in Fuccillo, Antonio (ed.), *Multireligiosità e reazione giuridica*, Giappichelli, Torino, 2008, 333–352.

Coglievina, Stella, "Italy", in Nielsen, Jørgen S. et al. (eds), *Yearbook of Muslims in Europe*, vol. 6, Leiden: Brill, 2014, pp. 334–351.

Colaianni, Nicola, "Alla ricerca di una politica del diritto sui rapporti con l'Islam (Carta dei valori e Dichiarazione di intenti)", *Stato, Chiese e pluralismo confessionale*, January 2009 (online journal, at www.statoechiese.it).

Colaianni, Nicola, "Musulmani italiani e Costituzione: il caso della Consulta islamica", *Quaderni di diritto e politica ecclesiastica*, 2006, no. 1, pp. 251–257.

Conti, Bartolomeo, *L'Islam en Italie. Les leaders musulmans entre intégration et séparation*, Paris: L'Harmattan, 2014.

Conti, Bartolomeo, « Les musulmans en Italie entre crise identitaire et réponses islamistes », *Revue Européenne des Migrations Internationales*, 27:2 (2011), pp. 183–201.

Conti, Bartolomeo, *Towards a pluralistic society: Good practices in the integration and social inclusion of Muslims in Italian cities*, EUI-Open Society Institute, 2013, at http://www.eui.eu/Projects/ReligioWest/Documents/Publications/REPORT2013CONTI.pdf.

D'Angelo, Giuseppe, "Uniformità della reazione ed incidenza delle differenziazioni territoriali: l'interpretazione «locale» del divieto di comparire «mascherati» in luogo pubblico al cospetto del valore costituzionale del diritto di libertà religiosa", in Fuccillo, Antonio (ed.), *Multireligiosità e reazione giuridica*, Giappichelli, Torino, 2008, 353–376.

Decaro Bonella, Carmela, *Tradizioni religiose e tradizioni costituzionali. L'islam e l'Occidente*, Rome: Carocci, 2013.

Doe, Norman, *Law and Religion in Europe: A Comparative Introduction*, Oxford: Oxford University Press, 2011.

Domianello, Sara, "Il pluralismo in materia religiosa nel settore matrimoniale", in Domianello, Sara (ed.), *Diritto e religione in Italia. Rapporto nazionale sulla salvaguardia della libertà religiosa in regime di pluralismo confessionale e culturale*, Bologna: il Mulino, 2012, pp. 113–137.

Fantelli, Paola, "La 'Dichiarazione di intenti per la federazione dell'Islam italiano': un primo commento", *Stato, Chiese e pluralismo confessionale*, online journal (www.statoechiese.it), 21 July 2008.

Ferrari, Alessandro, "A Besieged Right: Religious Freedom and the Italian War on the Burqa and the Niqab", in Ferrari, Alessandro, and Pastorelli, Sabrina (eds), *The Burqa Affair Across Europe. Between Public and Private Space*, Farnham: Ashgate, 2013, pp. 37–58.

Ferrari, Alessandro (ed.), *Islam in Europa/Islam in Italia tra dritto e società*, Bologna: Il Mulino, 2008.

Ferrari, Alessandro, "Islam in Italy: The 'Ghost' Religion (A 'non-religion' in a 'religious country')", *Annuaire Droit et Religions*, vol. 8, 2015–2016, pp. 365–382.

Ferrari, Alessandro, "Libertà religiosa e nuove presenze confessionali (ortodossi e islamici): tra cieca deregulation e super-specialità, ovvero del difficile spazio per la differenza religiosa", *Stato, Chiese e pluralismo confessionale*, online journal (www.statoechiese.it), 4 July 2011.

Ferrari, Alessandro, *La libertà religiosa in Italia. Un percorso incompiuto*, Rome: Carocci, 2012.

Ferrari, Alessandro, and Ferrari, Silvio, "Religion and the Secular State, The Italian Case" (Italian National Reports to Washington 2010), *The Cardozo Electronic Law Bulletin*, 16:1, Special Issue, available at http://cardozolawbulletin.blogspot.it/search/label/16.

Ferrari, Silvio, "La formazione degli imam", in Fondazione ISMU, *Quindicesimo rapporto sulle migrazioni 2009*, Milan: Franco Angeli, 2010, pp. 237–250.

Ferrari, Silvio, "The legal dimension", in Marechal, Brigitte et al. (eds.), *Muslims in the enlarged Europe: Religion and society*, Leiden: Brill, 2003, pp. 219–254.

Ferrari, Silvio, "Le moschee in Italia tra ordine pubblico e libertà religiosa", in Fondazione ISMU, *Quattordicesimo rapporto sulle migrazioni 2008*, Milan: Franco Angeli, 2009, pp. 219–236.

Ferrari, Silvio (ed.), *Musulmani in Italia. La condizione giuridica delle comunità islamiche*, Bologna: Il Mulino, 2000.

Ferrari, Silvio, "Religious entities as legal persons—Southern Europe (Cyprus, France,

Greece, Italy, Spain, Portugal)", in Friedner, Lars (ed.), *Churches and Other Religious Organisations as Legal Persons*, Proceedings of the 17th Meeting of the European Consortium for Church and State Research, Leuven: Peeters, 2007, pp. 21–26.

Ferrari, Silvio, and Bradney, Anthony (eds.), *Islam and European Legal Systems*, Farnham: Ashgate, 2000.

Finocchiaro, Francesco, *Diritto ecclesiastico*, Bologna: Zanichelli, 2012.

Fiorita, Nicola, "L'islam nei luoghi di lavoro: considerazioni introduttive sul ricorso alla contrattazione collettiva", *Coscienza e Libertà*, 39 (2005), pp. 9–19.

Fiorita, Nicola, and Tarchiani, Francesca, "L'Islam a Colle Val d'Elsa: pregi e difetti di un protocollo d'intesa", in http://www.olir.it/areetematiche/85/documents/Fiorita_Tarchiani_Islam_Colle.pdf.

Floris, Pierangela, "La tutela delle esigenze religiose in ambito locale tra regole giuridiche e buone pratiche. Il contesto italiano", in Castro Jover, Adoración (dir.), *Diversidad religiosa y gobierno local. Marco jurídico y modelos de intervención en España y en Italia*, Cizur Menor (Navarra): Thomson Reuters Aranzadi, 2013, pp. 175–206.

Frisina, Annalisa, *Giovani Musulmani d'Italia*, Rome: Carocci, 2007.

Gianfreda, Anna, "Libertà religiosa, spazi urbani e disciplina in materia di cimiteri e sepolture", in Chizzoniti, Antonio G. (ed.), *Religione e autonomie locali. La tutela della libertà religiosa nei territori di Cremona, Lodi e Piacenza*, Tricase (Le): Libellula Edizioni, 2014, pp. 108–136.

Guolo, Renzo, "Attori sociali e processi di rappresentanza nell'islam italiano", in Saint-Blancat, Chantal (ed.), *L'islam in Italia. Una presenza plurale*, Rome: Edizioni Lavoro, 1999.

Jasch, Hans-Christian, "State-Dialogue with Muslim Communities in Italy and Germany. The Political Context and the Legal Frameworks for Dialogue with Islamic Faith Communities in Both Countries", *German Law Journal*, 8:4, (2007), pp. 341–380.

Lerner, Pablo, and Rabello, Alfredo M., *Il divieto di macellazione rituale (shechità kosher e halal) e la libertà religiosa delle minoranze*, Padua: CEDAM, 2010.

Macrì, Gianfranco, "Brevi riflessioni sui pareri espresso dal Comitato per l'Islam italiano", *Quaderni di diritto e politica ecclesiastica*, 2012, n. 2, pp. 407–423.

Mancuso, Anna Sveva, *La rilevanza civile del matrimonio degli acattolici*, Rome: Edizioni Nuova Cultura, 2013.

Mancuso, Anna Sveva, "La presenza islamica in Italia: forme di organizzazione, profili problematici e rapporti con le istituzioni", *Stato, Chiese e pluralismo confessionale*, online journal (www.statoechiese.it), 22 February 2010.

Marchei, Natascia, "La legge della Regione Lombardia sull'edilizia di culto alla prova della giurisprudenza amministrativa", *Stato, Chiese e pluralismo confessionale*, online journal (www.statoechiese.it), 31 March 2014.

Musselli, Luciano, *Diritto e religione in Italia e in Europa. Dai concordati alla problematica islamica*, Turin: Giappichelli, 2011.

Naso, Paolo, and Salvarani, Brunetto (eds.), *Un cantiere senza progetto. L'Italia delle Religioni. Rapporto 2012*, Bologna: EMI, 2012.

Open Society Institute (OSI), *The Situation of Muslims in Italy*, Budapest: Open Society, 2002 (available at http://www.cestim.it/argomenti/02islam/osi%20-%20muslims%20in%20italy.pdf).

Pace, Enzo, and Frisina, Annalisa, "Italian Secularism Revisited? Muslims' Claims in the Public Sphere and the Long Struggle Towards Religious Equality", in Keskin, Tugrul (ed.), *Sociology of Islam. Secularism, Economy and Politics*, Reading: Ithaca Press, 2011, pp. 291–317.

Pacini, Andrea, *I musulmani in Italia*, Cestim, 2001 at http://www.cestim.it/argomenti/02islam/02islam-relazione-pacini.pdf.

Parisi, Marco, *Istruzione laica e confessionale nello Stato delle autonomie*, Naples: E.S.I., 2008.

Pastori, Giorgio, "Regioni e confessioni religiose nel nuovo ordinamento costituzionale", *Quaderni di diritto e politica ecclesiastica*, 2003, n. 1, pp. 3–12.

Petralia, Valentina, "Ricongiungimento familiare e matrimonio poligamico. Il riconoscimento di valori giuridici stranieri e la tutela delle posizioni deboli", *Università di Catania—Online Working Paper*, 2013, n. 49, at http://www.cde.unict.it/quadernieuropei/giuridiche/49_2013.pdf.

Rhazzali, Khalid, and Equizi, Massimiliana, "I musulmani e i loro luoghi di culto", in Pace, Enzo (ed.), *Le religioni nell'Italia che cambia*, Rome: Carocci. 2013, pp. 47–72.

Rivetti, Giuseppe, "Islam-Occidente. nuove identità religiose", in Picozza, Paolo, and Rivetti, Giuseppe (eds.), *Religione cultura e diritto tra globale e locale*, Milan: Giuffré, 2007, pp. 71–102.

Rocchini, Ylenia, "Matrimonio poligamico islamico e famiglie immigrate: l'esperienza giurisprudenziale italiana tra diritto privato e diritto pubblico", in Amram, Denise, and D'Angelo, Angela (eds.), *La famiglia e il diritto fra diversità nazionali ed iniziative dell'Unione Europea*, Padua: Cedam, 2011, pp. 279–300.

Saint-Blancat, Chantal, "Italy", in Cesari, Jocelyne (ed.), *The Oxford Handbook of European Islam*, Oxford: Oxford University Press, 2014, pp. 265–310.

Saint-Blancat, Chantal, and Schmidt di Friedberg, Ottavia, "Why are Mosques a Problem? Local Politics and Fear of Islam in Northern Italy", *Journal of Ethnic and Migration Studies*, 31:6 (2005), pp. 1083–1104.

Silvestri, Sara, "Institutionalizing British and Italian Islam: Attitudes and Policies", in Yilmaz, Hakan, and Aykaç, Çagla E. (eds.), *Perceptions of Islam in Europe: Culture, Identity and the Muslim "Other"*, London: I.B. Tauris, 2012, pp. 159–194.

Spreafico, Andrea, and Coppi, Andrea, "The Long Path from Recognition to Representation of Muslims in Italy", *The International Spectator, The journal of the Istituto Affari Internazionali* (IAI), 43:3 (2008), pp. 101–115.

Toronto, James A., "Islam Italiano: Prospects for Integration of Muslims in Italy's Religious Landscape", *Journal of Muslim Minority Affairs*, 28:1 (2008), pp. 61–82.

Tozzi, Valerio, and Macrì, Gianfranco (eds.), *Europa e Islam. Ridiscutere i fondamenti delle libertà religiose*, Soveria Mannelli: Rubbettino, 2009.

Ventura, Marco, "Religion and law in dialogue: Covenantal and non-covenantal cooperation of State and religions in Italy", in Puza, Richard, and Doe, Norman (eds.), *Religion and law in dialogue: Covenantal and non-covenantal cooperation between State and Religion in Europe*, Leuven: Peeters Publishers, 2006, pp. 115–129.

Ventura, Marco, *Religion and law in Italy*, Alphen an den Rijn: Wolters Kluwer International, 2013.

Vitali, Enrico, and Chizzoniti, Antonio G., *Diritto ecclesiastico. Manuale breve*, Milan: Giuffrè, 2015.

Zilio Grandi, Ida (ed.), *Il dialogo delle leggi. Ordinamento giuridico italiano e tradizione giuridica islamica*, Venice: Marsilio, 2006.

Zilio Grandi, Ida (ed.), *Sposare l'altro. Matrimoni e matrimoni misti nell'ordinamento italiano e nel diritto islamico*, Venice: Marsilio, 2006

Index